DIAKONIA

DIAKONIA

in the

CLASSICAL REFORMED TRADITION

and

TODAY

Elsie Anne McKee

WILLIAM B. EERDMANS PUBLISHING COMPANY
GRAND RAPIDS, MICHIGAN

Library of Congress Cataloging-in-Publication Data

McKee, Elsie Anne.
   Diakonia in the classical reformed tradition and today /
Elsie Anne McKee.
        p.   cm.
   Includes bibliographical references.
   ISBN 0-8028-0352-0
   1. Service (Theology)   2. Deacons—Reformed Church.
3. Reformed Church—Government.   4. Reformed Church—
Doctrines.   5. Reformed Church—Charities.   6. Reformed
Church—Liturgy.   I. Title.
BX9423.B45M35   1989
262'.1442—dc20   89-39372
                                                            CIP

for
MY PARENTS
and
SISTERS

CONTENTS

Contents

Contents

PREFACE

CHRISTIAN CONCERN for the suffering of the world is not a new development, but the church's role of providing service to the afflicted has sometimes been neglected. Individual Christians have frequently stood out as shining examples of self-forgetful compassion, and many more have labored quietly in their daily tasks to relieve the poor, sick, and oppressed. These individuals have frequently felt that the church has given them very little support, guidance, or even recognition.

There are a number of reasons for the development of confusion in the church's *diakonia*, literally, the church's ministry or service to the world. Perhaps one of the more significant is the individualist understanding of the church that influences much of post-Enlightenment Protestantism, especially in North America.

In recent decades, however, there has come a renewed appreciation of the corporate nature of the church as the Body of Christ, and with this renewal a fresh sense of what it means for the church as church to act in the world. The church is greater than the sum of its members. Believers do not form the church by agreeing together to incorporate; the church is the community into which individual Christians are baptized, a body of which they become members. One consequence of this reawakening to the corporate nature of the church has been a remarkable, ecumenical concern for the diaconal activity of the Body of Christ, and thus for the office of deacon. Many different Christian traditions have turned their attention to the study of the diaconate and have begun to reconsider their practice of it.

Before one can reform or even evaluate some part of life, whether individual or corporate, it is important to understand how present practices developed. What other ages have taught and done is not necessarily normative for the twentieth century, but failure to understand what we have inherited can make us puppets of the unknown past. It can also deny us the gifts of the faith and the wisdom of the communion of the saints.

This small book is offered to Christians of the Reformed tradition as an introduction to the classical Reformed diaconate and its context, a sketch of the development and meaning of the office of deacon in the sixteenth century. It is based in part on a more detailed study, my *John Calvin on the Diaconate and Liturgical Almsgiving* (Geneva, 1984), which was written as one contribution to the ecumenical investigation of the Christian diaconate. The purpose of this book is not primarily to provide a blueprint for twentieth-century ecclesiastical reform, although the final chapter offers some suggestions for contemporary practice. The objective of this book is to explain to contemporary Reformed deacons what their office originally meant, and to outline for individual Reformed Christians the corporate context in which their lives' service to the world may be understood. My hope is that seeing how the Reformed diaconate was conceived may spur twentieth-century Christians, both Reformed and ecumenical, to examine critically their own thought and practice, and to challenge them to serve God and God's people with ever greater faithfulness and wisdom in the present age.

I would like to express personal thanks: to my parents, Charles and Anne McKee, and to my sisters Beth, Kathy, and Charlene, for their example of unselfish *diakonia;* to several of my colleagues, friends, and students, especially professors John H.

Leith and George H. Sinclair, Jr., and Rev. Joyce Tucker, Elizabeth Killeen, John Morgan, and Arlene Nehring, who encouraged
me in my plan to write a book for the benefit of their own deacons. Ms. Killeen and Ms. Nehring were also kind enough to read
the manuscript, for which I am very grateful. I am deeply grateful, also, to Mr. Jon Pott, Dr. Charles Van Hof, Mr. Gary Lee, and
Ms. Ina Vondiziano, and others of William B. Eerdmans Publishing Company, for their helpfulness and courtesy, and for their
willingness to take a risk on a semipopular effort by a church-
woman-academic who does not want to be an "ivory tower!"

February 1988   E. A. McKee
Andover Newton   Tshimunyi wa Ngulumingi
Theological School

Introduction

THE PERPLEXING PRESENT

To work in the personal service of another human being is, once more, the least coveted role in human society. . . . It was scandalous for Jesus to interpret His own role, and to present the terms of discipleship, by using this model [of a domestic servant]. But He did so, with the personal service of the table-waiter firmly in view.

W. A. Whitehouse, "Christological Understanding"

In many churches there is today considerable uncertainty about the need, the rationale, the status and the functions of deacons.

Baptism, Eucharist, and Ministry[1]

OUR EXPERIENCE

A<small>N ELDERLY MAN</small> comes to his pastor with a request that she see about helping his neighbors, new members of the church. Their son is a quadriplegic and they need a van in which they can transport him to school and to the doctor. The pastor thanks the man for his awareness and suggests that he bring the problem to the deacons and ask them what can be done to help the family.

The youth group wants to have a hunger walk. They will ask the members of their church to sponsor them generously because they want to raise $1,000 for the starving children in the Sudan of whom their African classmate told them last week. Whom should they ask for help in organizing the effort? How can they send the money to the home church of their friend?

A social worker stands before her congregation during a "minute for mission" presentation. This week a young woman was referred to her after being arrested for selling drugs, which she did out of desperation because she did not know any other way to get food for her two babies. Where was the church when this woman needed help? Does the church care about the social worker's daily struggle to find hope for desperate people?

A college student appeals to his session to stand by him because he has been arrested for civil disobedience, protesting apartheid in South Africa. Some of the congregation are upset with the idea of nonviolent political action done in the name of Christ and Christ's church, although they all agree that apartheid is wrong and one must act on one's convictions. Are being a Christian and being part of the church two different things? Does the church as church have a responsibility for the bodies as well as the souls of human beings?

SOME OF OUR QUESTIONS

The relationship between religious faith and social responsibility is one of the most difficult questions for Christians, especially in our late twentieth-century world marked by complexity, ambiguity, and incredibly rapid change. The kinds of situations portrayed above are not unusual; they are part and parcel of the suffering, perplexing world in which all of us who want to be faithful Christians must live every day.

Poverty and need, whether next door or in the inner city or in Africa, are always with us. We realize that we are responsible for each other. Sometimes we forget, though, that our corporate response to need can be effective only if each person is alert to bring special concerns to the attention of the community and if we know to whom we can refer various kinds of problems. We often do not distinguish different kinds of ministry, and we may overwhelm pastors with everything or relegate deacons simply to building upkeep and finances. We are quick to respond to pleas for special projects, but we often do not have any clear idea of what channels exist for helping. We create ad hoc hunger committees or wait for information from the Red Cross or Oxfam or CROP. Our sense of oneness with fellow human beings suffering in other parts of the world is frequently somewhat tenuous because it may be dependent on haphazard contacts rather than having a clear focus in our own congregations. Yet some individuals in the congregation may daily serve the unfortunate, but because their jobs are paid by secular agencies we do not feel they represent the church and their ministry is not recognized or encouraged by the prayers of the whole church.

The problem is not even so simple as questions of ignorance of needs or ways and means to meet those needs. Sometimes more complicated theoretical issues are involved. Are we responsible only for charity, for humanity to the needy? Or should our vision of service be wider? Does the gospel address us only as individuals or also as a people?

Charity to a hungry family may not be controversial, but once the mother is arrested, what happens? Is there a role for the church in seeing that the drug-seller is treated with compassion and humanity as well as justice, and is trained to support herself and her children, rather than merely being punished? Venturing into questions of justice may be divisive, especially if a congregation does not have any clear theological sense of its corporate social responsibilities and the risky dimensions of loving the neighbor.

It may be possible to help a jailed divorcée and feed her children, but what about getting involved in civil disobedience? Even when the object of protest is plainly perceived as un-Christian, can or should the church as a body take a stand? If so, on what grounds? Within what limits? Is this optional or a matter of faith? If the latter, how might we go about educating ourselves and others so that living faithfully may be done by conviction and not merely by social pressure or grudging duty? What is the relationship of all this activity to the primary call of the church to proclaim the gospel? Is there any bridge between Sunday and the rest of the week? What does it mean that the church is called to *diakonia*, to the active love and service of the neighbor, that ministry includes work as well as worship?

Perplexing and frightening questions, indeed, but we are not the first to ask them, nor do we stand alone now. Over the centuries the Reformed tradition has earned a reputation for its social conscience, its concern for *diakonia*. This family of churches is known for an intense (if sometimes misguided) devotion to serving the will of God in *this* world as well as praying for the next, because the God known in Christ is adored as the redeemer of history, of the here and now as well as of eternity. Indeed, social action is usually and rightly considered a manifestation of faith in God. Nonetheless, the ties between justifying faith and public conscience have become nebulous for many. This is partly the result of living in a more complex society, particularly in the context of separation of church and state, in a nation which has long been influenced by Judeo-Christian ideals in its public life. The problem is also partly amnesia, however—forgetfulness of classical Reformed theology and the roots of the Reformed tradition's zeal for transforming culture.[2]

WHERE THIS BOOK IS GOING

Simply understanding the past will not tell us how to plan for the future, but it is a necessary first step. Different ages provide different opportunities and experience different limitations. Just as twentieth-century Christians enjoy the privileges and must deal with the constraints of the contemporary world, so those of every other age have had to seek the will of God in the context of the wisdom and limitations of their cultures.

The classical Reformed theology developed in an age with a religious worldview, a much stronger sense of biblical authority, and a less pluralistic society than ours. Nevertheless, if we recognize and make allowances for its differences, studying the past can provide one critical ingredient for analyzing and perhaps prescribing for the present. Experts in the dynamics of modern society must work with theologians to determine how the insights of the past may be reconceived and applied to serve our day, but first the roots of the tradition should be understood.

The present introduction to the classical Reformed diaconate begins by sketching the historical, theological, and social givens of its context. Who are the players and what does their stage look like? Chapter one describes the various reform movements, their view of the world and of civil-ecclesiastical relationships, the kinds of diversity developing in early modern society, and the understanding of the authority of Scripture. This material serves as a kind of framework for the diaconal story. Theology is a critical part of the stage, and chapter two provides an outline of the theoretical context for the Reformed concern for the poor. What is the relationship between worship and *diakonia,* between Sunday and the rest of the week? What were the traditional Protestant teachings on the ministry, and how did the Reformed doctrine of the plurality of ecclesiastical ministries, which includes the diaconate, develop? The next chapter considers the social scene, the practical context: the charitable practices of the late medieval period, and the changes of Renaissance social welfare reform, with special attention to the city-state of Geneva.

The central interest of the book is the teaching on the Reformed diaconate, which found its classical expression in the work of John Calvin. Calvin's doctrine is discussed as it developed in the various editions of his introduction to Scripture, *The Institutes of the Christian Religion,* and in his biblical commentaries and sermons. Special attention is focused on the biblical passages that the Reformer understood as the basis of his thought. The teaching on a twofold diaconate of men and women leads naturally into a consideration of the place Calvin accorded to women in this ministry and in the church's ministry more generally. This section of Calvin's thought looks toward the twentieth century for completion. One further historical chapter outlines some of the highpoints and difficulties in Protestant, especially Reformed, diaconal work, from Calvin's day to ours. This section concludes with a brief glance at the current discussions of the diaconate in the wider church; it draws particularly on the Faith and Order document *Baptism, Eucharist and Ministry,* and official responses to it.

The discussion of the *Baptism, Eucharist and Ministry* document brings the story full circle, back to the perplexing present. The final, nonhistorical part of the book is a suggestion for the use of the history. In chapter six I have ventured to sketch a portrait of what a Reformed diaconate might include in the late twentieth century. Although no one person can provide an adequate proposal for how modern churches might resolve the questions of responsibility for the temporal care of the neighbor, this is an issue which none of us can honestly avoid. The personal suggestions are offered simply as that, with the prayer that this whole experiment in drawing on the past to serve the future may be useful for the work of Christ's church in God's world.

Chapter One

THE PLAYERS AND THEIR STAGE

It was the best of times, it was the worst of times. . . .
Charles Dickens, *A Tale of Two Cities*[1]

WORDS WRITTEN ABOUT the cataclysm of the French Revolution are not inappropriately applied to the Renaissance and Reformations of the sixteenth century. In 1517 and for quite some time afterward, no one imagined that this was the beginning of a new age. And, indeed, no historical time is cut off from what goes before or comes after; the continuities are frequently stronger than the discontinuities. To understand the sixteenth century, as with any other period, however, it is sometimes useful to contrast it with what went before and what came after. In addition, to be able to use what we learn from any past age, it is important to understand the similarities to and differences from our own time.

AN AGE OF REFORMATIONS:
NAMING THE PLAYERS

The sixteenth century is well known as the age of Renaissance and Reformations, of a great rebirth of learning, both classical and religious. Rebirth within Christianity (as also in other religions) often means divisions. Those who call a people back to their sources are never fully accepted, and often the reformers do not agree among themselves on what needs changing or how it should be reconceived. It is for this reason that the word "Reformations" is used in the plural, and for this reason that the sixteenth century is known also as a time of religious division.[2]

There were a variety of different reformers and different ideals of reform in the early modern period. It is useful to identify the main characters and their ideas because different ideals of reform and different theologies had important consequences for the way various reformers envisioned and practiced *diakonia,* the service of church and individual Christian to the neighbor in need.

One ideal of religious reform is often labeled Christian or biblical humanism. Christian leaders in the rebirth we call the Renaissance were very much concerned with a return to the pure literary sources of the faith. They objected vigorously to the many accretions of pious imagination and scholastic theology, feeling that these things distracted people from a simple moral life of following Jesus' commands. Christian humanists, as they were called for their interest in the "humane" sciences (our liberal arts and humanities), contributed richly to the renewal of biblical and theological studies because they felt that proper education in the classics, especially teaching the golden rule, would reform society. Humanists not only objected to complicated theology and church ceremonies, but they also despised the confusion and clutter of the contemporary administration of charity. Moral reform meant social reform if the disorderly beggars were not to overwhelm Christian society.

Humanists often suggested more efficient ways to straighten out charitable problems. Many humanists remained Roman

Catholic, while many became Protestant. Both groups had in common a love of orderliness and simplicity, and a disgust with waste and inefficiency, and these characteristics contributed to new patterns of benevolence.

For another large group of reformers in the sixteenth century, the chief problem was not moral but theological and spiritual. Bad morals were a symptom, not the disease. What needed re-forming was the understanding of how one is saved. These "Protestants," led first by Martin Luther, are the best-known reformers of the period. Although none of the "protesters" began by wishing to organize separate Christian churches, they soon discovered that the established ecclesiastical authorities did not approve of the changes they believed were essential to right preaching of the faith.

Luther and his followers were convinced that what was needed was doctrinal reform, a revisioning of the meaning of Christian teaching, especially the doctrines of sin and grace. If salvation is by faith alone, and good works contribute nothing to it, then the reform of doctrine would have important implications for *diakonia*. As important as these implications were, they were not necessarily clear. For example, one might infer that people are free to forget charity, since salvation cannot be earned. Or one might believe that the necessary outflowing of gratitude for salvation would find expression in self-sacrifice for the neighbor. For Luther and his followers, of course, the latter was the correct conclusion to be drawn from justification by faith alone. This view was clearly expressed in Luther's famous treatise on Christian freedom.

> A Christian is a perfectly free lord of all, subject to none. A Christian is a perfectly dutiful servant of all, subject to all. . . .
>
> This is that Christian liberty, our faith, which does not induce us to live in idleness or wickedness but makes the law and works unncessary for any man's righteousness and salvation. . . . This is the place to assert that which was said above, namely, that a Christian is the servant of all and made subject to all. Insofar as he is free he does no works, but insofar as he is a servant he does all kinds of works.[3]

9

Almost all Protestants shared Luther's revision of the doctrine of grace and its consequences, but not all agreed on other questions of theological reform. Some of these differences led to divisions and even sometimes to hostility. Theological divergences not only marked different parties within Protestantism but also affected the development of the teaching and practice of *diakonia* or social service.

The major groups of Protestants besides Lutherans were those usually called the "Reformed," and those in the Church of England. The Swiss and South German Protestants led by Ulrich Zwingli felt that Luther and the "Lutherans" had retained too much of the Roman Catholic tradition. These "Zwinglians" or German-speaking "Reformed" differed from the Lutherans on a number of points, particularly the Lord's Supper and the application of *sola scriptura*, "Scripture alone." Nonetheless, Zwingli, like Luther, retained a clear sense of Christendom as a whole, including both ecclesiastical and civil authorities in one society.

Certain reformers who had strong sympathies with both Luther and Zwingli eventually developed two more major streams of Protestantism. One of these very influential groups was led initially by Martin Bucer, though its most important leader was John Calvin, whose name was adopted for the whole "Calvinist Reformed" tradition. Although Bucer and Calvin shared many of Luther's theological emphases, Lutherans and Calvinists grew further apart and Zwinglians and Calvinists closer together, until in 1549 Calvin and Zwingli's successor Heinrich Bullinger agreed to share the Lord's Supper together. This union of Zwinglians and Calvinists became known as the "Reformed" branch of Protestantism. Theological differences within the tradition were not eliminated, however, and Reformed Protestants continued to be more diverse than Lutherans.[4] The Church of England, which also combined Lutheran and Reformed streams of influence, is often seen as the third main branch of Protestantism. By the later sixteenth century much of English theology was Reformed, but the church's polity continued to be more traditional.

Calvinist Reformed, like Zwinglians, interpreted *sola scrip-*

tura more strictly than did Lutherans, but they also envisioned the relationship between civil and ecclesiastical authorities differently from German-speaking Protestants, Lutheran or Zwinglian, and this point had important consequences for the diaconal structure developed in Calvinist church orders.

Still another ideal of reform was advocated and practiced by some individuals and small groups in the sixteenth century. These scattered reformers are sometimes called "Radicals" because of their desire to return to the roots *(radices)* of the faith.[5] For these people, reform was not enough; the whole of Christendom was an affront to the God of the New Testament. What was needed was not mere reform but a true restoration of the early Christian community. Less concerned with doctrinal reform than other Protestants, most Radicals, like Christian humanists, were concerned chiefly for moral reform, although they usually sought it primarily through disciplined communal life rather than individual education. The major, organized communities of Radicals, sometimes called "Anabaptists" for their practice of adult or believer's baptism, regarded Scripture as the root to which the church must be restored. Concentrating almost exclusively on the New Testament, Anabaptists criticized Lutheran and Reformed Protestants because they felt the latter had compromised with the wicked world. According to the Radicals, Protestant churches made little or no effort to separate the wheat from the chaff, the elect from the reprobate, the church from the world (or state).

Strict focus on the New Testament and rejection of the world had many consequences for Radical thought and practice, not least for the attitudes to *diakonia*. Copying the New Testament did not always or even normally mean that Anabaptists practiced communal ownership, but general fear of this interpretation of the book of Acts contributed to persecution of the Radicals. Further, Anabaptists considered government social programs a travesty of Christian charity, and thus dissociated themselves from contemporary welfare reforms.

Reform was not confined to those who broke with Rome; movements of renewal were also strong within Roman Catholicism. Some of these reforms were essentially continuous with late medieval and Christian humanist efforts at moral change and personal devotion; others were clearly reactions to the challenges of Protestantism. A vigorous effort was made to bring the faith closer to ordinary people, to evangelize nominal Catholics and those who had fallen away to Protestantism. Roman Catholic doctrine was restated, clarified, and made uniform by the Council of Trent (1545-1563), but the teaching was not fundamentally altered. Ecclesiastical abuses were curbed, and the organization of the church, including the traditional teachings and practice of *diakonia*, were reaffirmed and strengthened to resist threats from both within and without. (Indeed, it might be said that the Roman church in the later sixteenth century was girded for battle.) Reform was moral and disciplinary, but it did not meet Protestant demands for theological renewal, and thus the world of Western Christendom was broken into pieces, at first a few and then more and more.

SIXTEENTH- AND TWENTIETH-CENTURY WORLDVIEWS

How we look at things, the unconscious assumptions of our age and our culture, have a very powerful influence on the ways we act, on what we consider possible or impossible, necessary or insignificant. If we want to understand the relationship between two things, such as belief in God and honesty in dealing with other people, we must understand not only the things themselves but also their context, how they are related in one overall picture. This comprehension can be particularly difficult if the things are very familiar to us. It is hard to remember that another age or culture might affirm the same things we do but organize the relationship between them somewhat differently. The worldviews of the sixteenth and twentieth centuries have many common elements but rather different contexts, and these differences affect strongly the conception and practice of *diakonia*.

Although sometimes the sixteenth century is considered

the beginning of modern times, with all that that implies of secularism, individualism, and rationalism, the age of Reformations in some ways had more in common with the preceding age of faith than the philosophical age of reason which followed. The religious, intellectual, and social changes of the sixteenth century were marked, but in many ways the continuities of the era strike modern eyes more forcibly than the discontinuities. Looking back across the great divide of the eighteenth-century Enlightenment, with all it brought both of freedom and fragmentation, we have a very difficult time comprehending a religious worldview.

What was this religious worldview of Reformation Christians which we find so distant and hard to understand? Most simply put, the sixteenth century in general shared the assumption of earlier Christendom that the God revealed in Christ is the ultimate authority in all spheres of life; there is no other basis of values, whether in work or worship. No aspect of human life is autonomous; whether practiced faithfully or honored in the breach, religious teaching is seen as relevant to every human activity.

The religious worldview of sixteenth-century Christians can perhaps best be illustrated by contrast with our own secular worldview. Twentieth-century people (at least in the West) tend to divide life into compartments, into common (or secular) and Christian realms. There is a public sphere in which the highest ethical norm may be "honesty is the best policy," and there is the narrow private space in which we hope to approximate the golden rule. Our society assumes that religious faith may give people guidance for their personal relationships, their "private" lives. However, most of the modern West believes that the economic and political "public" realms include all kinds of people who can only be expected to cooperate on the basis of purely natural values, a lowest-common-denominator kind of morality.

In contrast, sixteenth-century Christians simply assumed that God's will, however it was determined, was the basis for all of life. Whether the medium for knowing God's will was

13

church teaching (Roman Catholics) or Scripture (Protestants) or direct revelation (some Radicals), no one questioned that every aspect of a Christian's life should be redeemed and ordered by God and is responsible to God. There is no sphere of life in which the revealed will of God is not relevant and normative. A beautiful passage from Calvin's *Institutes of the Christian Religion* illustrates this point well.

> We are not our own: let not our reason nor our will, therefore, sway our plans and deeds. We are not our own: let us therefore not set it as our goal to seek what is expedient for us according to the flesh. We are not our own: in so far as we can, let us therefore forget ourselves, and all that is ours.
>
> Conversely, we are God's: let us therefore live for him and die for him. We are God's: let his wisdom and will therefore rule all our actions. We are God's: let all the parts of our life accordingly strive toward him as our only lawful goal [Rom. 14:8; cf. 1 Cor. 6:19].[6]

One of the important implications of the religious worldview for *diakonia* is the assumption that all Christians, all people, are obligated to love their neighbors, because all accept this service as God's will. Disagreement arose over how *diakonia* was to be practiced and especially who was responsible for its public leadership, but no one doubted that every Christian — and this usually meant every member of society — was to live charitably as a duty owed to God. In the twentieth century, a strong humanitarian impulse is found in many people, but even many Christians do not automatically regard the marketplace, the government office, the union meeting, the expressway, as being governed by the same principles that they acknowledge in personal relationships. There are certainly some benefits in this breakdown of a monolithic approach to morality. The gain in tolerance, however, seems balanced by a fragmentation in coherence which is manifested in our groping to grasp what, if any, relationship exists between Sunday and Monday, between our private lives and our political, economic, and social communities.

14

ECCLESIASTICAL-CIVIL OR
CHURCH-STATE RELATIONS

One of the most obvious differences between the sixteenth and
twentieth centuries is the problem posed by the relating of the
two key authorities in our common life, the religious and the
secular, or church and state. In the twentieth-century West,
especially in North America, the words "church" and "state"
conjure up two distinct institutions. It may seem sometimes that
Christians are born into both, but a glance at the world around
us reminds us that, from a legal viewpoint, we are necessarily
born only into the civil community, not also the religious.

In the sixteenth century this distinction did not hold.
Rather than seeing the church as a separate institution to which
one might or might not belong, a religious worldview assumes
the applicability of religious as well as civil authority to everyone
in the society. How a religious worldview is practiced may well
vary, though, depending on how the society is defined and how
the different callings (vocations) in that society are valued. The
various conceptions of both society and the vocations have important consequences for *diakonia*.

The least typical interpretation of the sixteenth-century
religious worldview, that of the Radical or Anabaptist reformers,
focused on redefining the community. Many Radicals believed
that all of Christian life must be regulated by strict adherence
to the New Testament. According to their understanding of the
latter, Christians should not take part in civil government or use
the sword, which is necessary to control sinful society. Thus the
true church, ruled in every detail of its life by the revealed will
of God, must withdraw from the unredeemed world. In some
ways, the Anabaptist Radicals' worldview had certain similarities with the modern split between religious and secular, although they by no means shared the modern toleration of those
who live "in the world." Radicals did not divide their own lives
into religious and secular compartments, but they segregated
their religious society from the unregenerate world around
them. In theory all Christian activities were valued equally,

15

whether one cared for temporal needs or preached the gospel. Some Anabaptist communities had special leadership for diaconal work. Sometimes, though, such distinctions were not made, and the communal leadership (in consultation with the whole body) handled all questions, marriage and apprenticeships, sacraments and missionary work, cooking responsibilities and child-rearing rules.

For most sixteenth-century Christians, however, Christendom was still a reality; the question was not the limits of Christian society but the relationship of different callings, especially ecclesiastical and civil authorities, within the one Body of Christ. For Roman Catholics, the issue was the relative value of spiritual (ecclesiastical) and temporal (civil) vocations in a Christian society. For Protestants, it was rather a matter of the relationship between different, equally religious callings. To the medieval and sixteenth-century Roman Catholic Christian, the highest representative of God on earth was the visible church, with the pope as its head and the clergy as its local leaders. The ecclesiastical was superior to the civil; both were established by God but the civil had a derivative authority mediated through the church. The ecclesiastical was usually identified with the holy, the civil with the profane. Bishops, priests, deacons, and other ministers, monks, and nuns were considered to have religious callings because they were dedicated to the church, while housewives, tailors, farmers, mothers, and even princes lived "in the world." All could be faithful Christians, but spiritual duties had intrinsically a higher value than temporal ones.

For Lutheran, Reformed, and Church of England Protestants, however, the doctrine of justification by faith alone eliminated any essential distinctions among Christians. There are no privileged Christians with special access to God; all within the priesthood of believers are called to vocations which are equally religious in that they honor God and serve the neighbor. Social differences remained, but the wall between sacred and profane was redefined; what mattered now was faith or unbelief, not ecclesiastical or worldly callings. The place of the holy was shifted from a sacred space to the world, or this age *(saeculum)*, that is, the whole of human life. Thus, while Protestants, like most other Christians, affirmed vigorously that God is the ultimate Lord of both ecclesiastical and civil spheres, they no longer subordinated the latter to the former. God has directly established each power to have authority in its own tasks, both ministers and magistrates to care for the varied needs of God's people. It is obvious that the revaluing of the "worldly," the nonecclesiastical, would have a very great impact on the way Protestants understood the status of *diakonia*. Temporal care for the poor was no longer less religious than ecclesiastical activity.[7]

The revaluing of the worldly, the secular, the lay, is often seen as an important impetus or contribution given by Protestantism to the development of the modern worldview. This is both true and false, since the words "secularization" and "laicization" apply differently to the sixteenth and twentieth centuries. Protestants secularized the world in the sense that they denied a hierarchy of ecclesiastical over civil/temporal, but never in the modern sense of building (part if not all of) their lives on some other authority than the will of God. Protestants laicized the world in the sense of eliminating essential religious distinctions among Christians, but not in the sense of saying that lay and ordained are independent of each other.

Protestants did not agree among themselves, however, on how the ecclesiastical and civil authorities established by God are related to each other, and this disagreement had significant consequences for the official leadership of Christian *diakonia*. Some Protestants, for example, Lutherans, Zwinglian Reformed, and most Anglicans, concluded that the ecclesiastical is concerned only with the preaching of the Word and the administration of the sacraments. The civil (which is still a *religious* authority because God established earthly rulers) is responsible for all the other practical, administrative affairs of the church as well as of the state.

For Reformed leaders like John Oecolampadius and Martin Bucer, John Calvin and John Knox, however, the role of the ecclesiastical includes more than just the ministry of Word and

17

sacraments. These Calvinist Reformed believed that the church must have its own organization, it must have autonomy not only in the ministry of Word and sacraments but also in the moral oversight of the congregation (including who may take the Lord's Supper). The ecclesiastical authority has the responsibility and therefore must have the power to correct its members, to provide for their care when they are poor or sick, and to teach them. Some of these duties might be shared with the civil authority in a Christian society; when the Holy Spirit inspires in princes and magistrates a concern for justice and righteousness, this work must be appreciated. Nonetheless, the church must acknowledge, and must be free to carry out, ministries of discipline, relief for the poor, and education. Thus, for the Calvinist Reformed, the roles of the ecclesiastical and civil authorities were divided in a slightly different way than for other Protestants, with Calvinists assigning a greater number of roles to the ecclesiastical ministry.

The ecclesiastical-civil relationships of sixteenth-century Christians can be sketched in contrast to the twentieth-century separation of church and state. Modern Christians clearly recognize religious pluralism as a fact and even a value; religious groups are independent of the state and the latter is ecclesiastically, if not ethically, neutral. (Separation of church and state does not always mean separation of religion and state, a point which can be confusing to those who have difficulty distinguishing between being Christian and being religious.) However, no sixteenth-century group except perhaps the Anabaptists could envision a world in which religious and civil communities were not coterminous. The internal relationships between civil and ecclesiastical might and did vary from one group of Christians to another, but the conviction that a community should have a common faith as well as a common government was rarely challenged. Civil and ecclesiastical authorities often experienced tension regarding their proper spheres, but some form of cooperation was seen as natural and essential.

SOCIETY IN THE EARLY MODERN WORLD

Religious teaching is always conditioned in some ways by its historical and social contexts. As Christians, people who worship a God who took history seriously enough to enter it personally, we must not only weigh carefully the influence of social, political, and economic factors on the expression and practice of faith, but we must also not see these influences as necessarily a threat. Thus it is important to understand something about the practical world in which a doctrine is taught. In the present case that means knowing something about the similarities and differences between the sixteenth-century world and our own, in order to appreciate and appropriate what the past can teach us about living our common faith responsibly.[8]

No society is completely homogeneous, but pluralism of all kinds has especially flourished in the modern world. The Renaissance is sometimes seen as the beginning of the significant and increasing cultural diversity which has produced the rich and sometimes bafflingly complex global village in which we live. The degree of social change in the sixteenth century may seem tame to us, but it was perplexing and sometimes even terrifying to those who experienced it.

The relative uniformity of late medieval society was beginning to break up even before the religious unity of Western Christendom was visibly split by the Protestant Reformation. The stable social order of feudalism had been crumbling for some time, with consequences especially for economic and cultural but also for political life. Increased and expanded trade brought the rise of cities and a small middle class. As traditional ties weakened, the appeal of freedom in the new urban centers grew. Great suffering and tension were apparent, especially in the rural areas, where the bulk of the population lived and where peasant revolts were increasingly common. Despite greater diversification within society, no one questioned the principle of hierarchical organization in the structure of civil life (though Protestants would challenge the *essential* character of ecclesiastical hierarchy). It was clear, however, that society was

19

changing, and not all for the better. How different groups envisioned a just social order varied, though, and the variations would influence both the ideals and the shape of change.

Contradictory intellectual interests of the Renaissance also affected the social tensions of the early modern world. More travel and education for at least a small number of people contributed to the cosmopolitan character of the elite, especially in humanist circles, but there was also an opposite cultural pull, a growing tendency toward national consciousness. (Although some centralization of governments was evident, for example, in England, the new awareness of being "German" or "French" must not be confused with a modern idea of nationality. The allegiances were often more linguistic and cultural than political.) The ties among religious reformers were influenced by linguistic and cultural boundaries, while the breaking up of Christendom into nations in turn often followed the lines of religious division created by the Reformations.

Religious controversy in the sixteenth century divided Christendom into competing confessional territories, but it did not mean that different faiths were permitted in the same jurisdiction. Pluralism extended to the point that different understandings of Christianity were found in different parts of Europe, but only one interpretation was allowed in any given place. Nonetheless, for sixteenth-century people to be confronted with more than one way of worshiping God, more than one way of being Christian, was undoubtedly as upsetting and confusing to them as having many religions in one society is to modern people. Perhaps it was even worse, since the twentieth century as a whole does not take religion nearly as seriously as did that earlier age.

Thus the sixteenth century, like the twentieth, was dealing with tumultuous upheaval in society. Much more homogeneous from our point of view than our own time, the age of the Reformations was experiencing social, cultural, economic, political, and religious changes which strained to the limit the human capacity to cope. This upheaval was especially true for Protestants, who were having to carve out a largely new way of grounding as well as of organizing their society. In a time when the will of God was understood as relevant for every sphere of life, a major challenge to traditional religious authority was critical for the whole social order.

SOLA SCRIPTURA AND ITS APPLICATION

A major challenge to traditional religious authority is perhaps one of the most succinct ways of describing the Protestant Reformations. The whole question of authority is difficult in any age of rapid change, and a problem of religious authority cannot avoid being cataclysmic in a society with a religious worldview.

In the course of human history religion has been based on a variety of authorities. The most common in Christian history have been the Bible, reason, tradition, and religious or mystical experience. Often these sources of authority have been combined, for example, reason or tradition or experience with Scripture. In modern times reason in the form of science has become the dominant form of authority for many people, while others have countered empiricism with mysticism and claimed their personal experience as the final authority.

In the Judeo-Christian tradition the Bible has, of course, always been prized as the Word of God, but the Bible does not explain everything human beings want to know about religion. Thus, for example, in the Middle Ages philosophical reason had become a second important source of church teaching, contributing to the formulation of tradition and the filling in of logical gaps in biblical revelation. Although Protestants challenged the church and rejected medieval theology on a number of grounds, most often the issue was whether the church can be the infallible interpreter of Scripture, whether the Bible can or needs to be supplemented by human reason or tradition.

It is common knowledge that *sola scriptura* (Scripture alone) was the cry of the Protestant reformers. What this meant in the context of the sixteenth century has sometimes not been as clearly remembered. Scripture has always been a crucial or even the ultimate authority for Christians, but it has not always

21

been their *sole* authority. For medieval Christians, the church had come to play an important role as the authoritative, indeed, infallible, interpreter of the Bible. In addition, over time a number of extrabiblical traditions had developed; these traditions had been handed down from age to age as apostolic, and by the late Middle Ages they were coming to be considered a separate source of revelation. (This so-called two-source theory, expressed in much more nuanced and guarded fashion, was decreed to be a dogma of the church by the Council of Trent in 1546.) Protestants retained a very high regard for the teaching role of the church; they were by no means advocates of an individualistic private judgment. They did, however, deny that the church can claim an infallible understanding of Scripture. Protestants thus continued to use tradition and reason, in various ways and to different degrees, but they rejected any claims of a supplemental revelation or definitive interpretation. Martin Luther's ideas for Christian educational reform point clearly to this elevation of the Bible to a rank apart.

> Even the writings of any one of the holy Fathers or, indeed, all of them, should only be read for a while, and in order that they might lead us to the Bible. Today, however, we read them alone, and get no further; we never enter on the Bible. Thus we are like those who look at the sign-posts, but never set out on the journey. The intention of the early Fathers in their writing was to introduce us to the Bible; but we use them only to find a way of avoiding it. . . .
>
> Above all, the most important and most usual teaching, in both the universities and the lower schools, ought to be concerned with the Holy Scriptures; beginning with the gospels for young boys. Would to God also that each town had a girls' school where, day by day, the girls might have a lesson on the gospel, whether in German or Latin.[9]

Thus Protestants, while not rejecting the use of other aids to its understanding, insisted that Scripture is not only the ultimate but also the sole authority.

If the Bible is the sole authority, what makes it authoritative and for what is it authoritative? In modern times these questions have been fiercely argued. Historical-critical studies have led to new ways of reading Scripture. Sometimes they have challenged the accuracy of the biblical narratives and claims, and said that this collection of books is not the direct communication of God with human beings but a series of documents recording human religious experience. More commonly, scholars have recognized that the Scriptures, which are human documents as well as divine revelation, are not a single whole. The new awareness of the diversity adds a dimension of richness previously lacking, but it can complicate the application of the teaching.

The sixteenth-century Christian did not consciously analyze what made the Bible authoritative; no one questioned that this was God's Word to human beings. There was relatively minor disagreement on the exact limits of the canon (what books belong in the Bible). On the one hand, some Radicals supplemented Scripture with visions inspired by the Spirit, in much the same way that Roman Catholics used tradition. On the other hand, many Protestants relegated the Apocrypha (books found in the Greek Old Testament but not the Hebrew) to a secondary status, while Radicals and Roman Catholics kept the whole. Martin Luther did have doubts about certain books (for example, the epistle of James), but generally there was no reason to question the literal inspiration of the text. The ordinary fashion of quoting Scripture, especially in polemical contexts, was a proof-texting method which recognized no difference between what modern scholars have called revelation and inspiration, the Christocentric message of salvation found in Scripture and the way the words got onto the page.[10]

Martin Luther and John Calvin, however, seem in some ways to have been exceptions to this general rule. While holding to the inspiration of the whole canon of the Bible, Luther and Calvin based the authority of Scripture on its revelation of redemption in Jesus Christ. This idea is never clearly articulated, but both Reformers appear to have distinguished between the revelation in and the letters of the text. Luther's words to Erasmus in *On the Bondage of the Will*, while focused primarily

23

on how to interpret obscure passages of Scripture, suggest this Christocentricity.

> I certainly grant that many *passages* in the Scriptures are obscure and hard to elucidate, but that is due, not to the exalted nature of their subject, but to our own linguistic and grammatical ignorance; and it does not in any way prevent our knowing all the *contents* of Scripture. For what solemn truth can the Scriptures still be concealing, now that the seals are broken, the stone rolled away from the door of the tomb, and that greatest of all mysteries brought to light—that Christ, God's Son, became man, that God is Three in One, that Christ suffered for us, and will reign for ever? And are not these things known, and sung in our streets? Take Christ from the Scriptures—and what more will you find in them?[11]

The reformers' view of revelation and inspiration in turn influenced their answers to the question of what Scripture is intended to teach. For Luther and Calvin, Scripture was not a scientific textbook but the source of the knowledge of redemption and the new life God wants Christians to live. Calvin emphasized that Scripture is accommodated to human understanding, God speaking to human children in baby talk. (God's condescension to human beings as a nurse to small children does not mean that the language of Scripture is untrue but that it is suited to the capacity of the hearers rather than expressed in the way the members of the Trinity might communicate among themselves.) In addition, Luther and Calvin knew that the Bible as a book has no power in itself. It only becomes authoritative in a personal way for the individual Christian by what Calvin calls the internal testimony of the Holy Spirit, which illuminates the mind and seals the truth of revelation in the believer's heart.[12]

If we leave aside the modern problem of inspiration, and grant that the Bible was the sole and unquestioned source of *revelation* for all Protestants and many Radicals, how the authority of Scripture was applied varied. Indeed, *sola scriptura* could be interpreted in several ways. According to what may be designated the Lutheran view, the sole authority of Scripture meant that anything contrary to the Bible must go, but other historical developments which have not been abused are welcome as part of the Christian heritage. For more austere critics like the Reformed, usually only what is found in or can be plainly inferred from Scripture is warranted. For Anabaptist Radicals, Scripture, especially the New Testament, is a model to be copied in every detail for the restoration of the apostolic church.

The consequences of these different views of the applicability of Scripture may be suggested more clearly in the following way. All who accepted *sola scriptura* agreed that the Bible is the only source of doctrine, but beyond that point differences began to emerge. For Lutherans, doctrine was to be drawn from Scripture, but other aspects of Christian life, including how *diakonia* is to be organized, were based on doctrine plus other circumstances of Christian history and present need. For Anabaptists, Scripture was seen as the precise pattern not only for doctrine but also for every facet of Christian life, from speech and dress to economy and pacifism. Naturally, *diakonia* was also ordered by Scripture, and some Anabaptists instituted communal ownership on the model of Acts 4:32ff. The Reformed interpretation stood more or less between these extremes, seeing Scripture as the guide to the right ordering of Christian worship, church government, and *diakonia,* as well as the source of doctrine, but not making the Bible a rigid blueprint for every detail of social existence.

Thus a comparison of the givens of the sixteenth and twentieth centuries presents many similarities and perhaps more differences. The first Protestants lived in a religious world, in a society in which ecclesiastical and civil authorities were part of one conceptual universe, in a time when very few people seriously questioned the truth or ultimate authority of the Bible. Our secular age, with its religious pluralism and separation of church and state, its empiricism and fundamental relativism, seems very far removed from such a view. We do share, however, the Protestant conviction that this age, this world, is the sphere in which we are called to live as Christians. Like sixteenth-century Christians, we live in an era of great upheaval and rapid change, and we share the problems of trying to comprehend and do what is faithful in our time and place. Having compared and contrasted some of the differences of historical circumstances between Calvin's day and ours, we can now study more closely the theological and social contexts in which the classical Reformed diaconate was developed.

Chapter Two

THE THEOLOGICAL CONTEXT

When during World War II the Netherlands were occupied by Germany the deacons of the Dutch Reformed Church assumed the care for the politically persecuted, supplying food and providing secret refuge. Realizing what was happening, the Germans decreed that the elective office of the deacon should be eliminated. The Reformed Synod on 17 July 1941 resolved: "Whoever touches the diaconate interferes with what Christ has ordained as the task of the Church. He touches the cult of the Church." Whoever lays hands on diakonia lays hands on worship! The Germans backed down. In taking diakonia seriously in a concrete political situation the Church begins to grasp her very being.

F. Herzog, "Diakonia in Modern Times"[1]

MANY OF US are acquainted with people who seem content to practice their Christianity on Sunday, and with others who give of themselves generously in their daily lives while rejecting any need for corporate worship. Sometimes we ourselves grope to explain how our communal prayer is related to our lives Monday through Saturday, and we may even feel that the connection is tenuous and unsatisfying at best. Others before us have struggled with these tensions. Some of their ideas and actions may at least provide food for thought, if not suggestions for concrete solutions to the problem.

THE RELATIONSHIP OF WORSHIP AND ETHICS

From its birth in the matrix of the Jewish covenant people, the Christian church has shared the mother people's sense of a corporate identity as the people of God. Much of the Christian faith is molded by its Hebraic heritage. This is especially true with regard to the church's understanding of service: the service of God (*leitourgia,* worship), and the service of the neighbor (*diakonia,* love). The ministry of the church is service, first to God and then to the neighbor, the one flowing inevitably from the other. Because (perhaps especially in modern times) the wholeness of the Judeo-Christian vision of *leitourgia-diakonia* has become difficult to explain clearly, it is helpful to see how the classical Reformed tradition defined the relationship between worship and ethics.[2]

Fundamental to all of Protestant theology is the doctrine of faith alone through grace, the conviction that we as sinners estranged from God have—amazingly!—been forgiven and accepted as if we possessed Christ's righteousness. Justification by faith alone through grace means not that we are, or ever in this life can be, worthy of God's love, but that God has counted us acceptable simply for Christ's sake. We receive this gift by faith, which is the work of the Holy Spirit making us trust that God in fact means all the promises of mercy. This incredible gift fills us with energy, with a need to respond in gratitude. Standing now freed of all condemnation, the justified, accepted sinner cannot help wanting to praise God. Nor can the praise of God be confined to words; everyone must share in the wonderful news and everyone's suffering must be healed because Christ came "to preach good news to the poor, . . . to proclaim release to the captives and recovering of sight to the blind, to set at liberty those who are oppressed, to proclaim the acceptable year of the Lord" (Luke 4:18-19, quoting Isa. 61:1, 2; 58:6 [RSV]).

The redeemed sinner wants above all to please God simply out of gratitude, but how do we know what pleases God? Many Christians believe that the church father Augustine of Hippo was right when he said: "Love [God], and do what thou wilt."[3] Reformed Christians, however, have always taught that, although Augustine is essentially correct, in the law God has provided us with a more precise guide for how to love our neighbors. The law must be rightly understood, though. Unlike Martin Luther, who thought that the two functions of law were to accuse and to restrain sinners, John Calvin and other Reformed theologians held that a "third use" of the law is primary. For the regenerate child of God, the original and true purpose of the law is to serve as a structure for living a redeemed life; it is a framework for love and justice. For Calvinists the sequence is gospel first, then law, because justification by Christ's grace is the beginning of true life. The third use of the law follows, then, to guide the faithful in right living.

The structure of right living given by the law echoes the golden rule, one of the first lessons a Christian child learns. The two chief obligations of the Christian can be summed up in the words of Christ, "You shall love the Lord your God with all your heart, and with all your soul, and with all your mind, and with all your strength. . . . You shall love your neighbor as yourself" (Mark 12:30-31 [RSV]). These two commands also express the essence of the two tables of the Decalogue (laws one through four, five through ten), and John Calvin often reduces the golden rule to two words or phrases: *pietas*, "piety, devotion" (or "obligations, duties of piety, devotion"), and *caritas*, "love" (or "obligations. . . , duties of love"). He sometimes uses a number of other words, such as "faith," "worship/service," "fear of God" for *pietas*, or "righteousness," "integrity," "humanity" for *caritas*. Sometimes balanced expressions, such as "the rule of living devoutly and justly," serve as synonyms. The paired themes of *pietas* and *caritas* run like shining threads throughout Calvin's writings.[4]

It is clear, then, that the regenerate life of the justified sinner has two principal foci: God and the neighbor. In view of the nature of these two objects, it is obvious that the two principal obligations of the Christian are not on an equal footing, but they are inseparable. The worship of God always takes precedence in importance, the love of the neighbor is the subordinate but *inevitable* corollary. In fact, love and justice for the neighbor (that is, for any human being!)[5] are usually the best evidence of our adoration of God. The faith which justifies us gives birth to both worship and love, but it is more unmistakably expressed in caring for our neighbors than in the ceremonies of outward worship. In principle, corporate services of praise have first claim. Because gestures can be a cover for hypocrisy, however, our treatment of our neighbors is usually a better measure of the true worship of the heart. Commenting on Galatians 5:14, "For the whole law is fulfilled in one word, even in this: Thou shalt love thy neighbour as thyself," Calvin provides a succinct summary of his teaching on the third use of the law, the relationship between worship and ethics.

> While they insisted on ceremonies alone, Paul glances in passing at the true duties and exercises of Christians. The present commendation of love is intended to teach the Galatians that it forms the chief part of Christian perfection. But we must see why all the precepts of the law are comprehended under love. The law consists of two tables, the first of which teaches of the worship of God and the duties of godliness and the second of love. . . . Piety towards God is, I confess, higher than love of the brethren; and therefore the observance of the first table is more valuable in the sight of God than that of the second. But as God Himself is invisible, so godliness is something hidden from the human senses. And although the ceremonies were appointed to bear witness to it, they are not certain proofs. It often happens that none are more zealous and regular in observing ceremonies than hypocrites. God therefore wants to make trial of our love to Him by that love of our brother which He commends to us. This is why not here alone, but also in Rom. 13:8 and 10, love is called the fulfilling of the law. . . . Love to men springs only from the fear and love of God. Therefore it is not surprising if by synecdoche the effect includes under it the cause of which it is the sign. But it would be wrong to separate the love of God from the love of men.[6]

To say that for Calvin love is better evidence of regeneration than formal worship is not to denigrate the critical importance of the proclamation of the revelation in Scripture. It does mean that the Reformer took with absolute seriousness the concern for the neighbor. The glory of God, the honoring of the awesome grace of Christ, had first place for Calvin, and theologians have often discussed the Reformer as if nothing else mattered to him. Inseparably linked with the concern for the worship of God was, however, its fruit: the love of the neighbor. This point must be remembered, since the tendency to split Calvin's theology into pieces is one major source of modern Reformed confusion on the relationship of worship and ethics.[7]

THE LITURGICAL CONTEXT OF *DIAKONIA*

One important way to demonstrate the essential connection between *pietas* and *caritas,* between liturgy and service, is to examine the classical Reformed paradigm for proper corporate worship. The Protestant Reformation was in a way fully as much a reform of worship as of theology; the critical question is the right praise of God, and all which does not truly glorify God must be eliminated. (Although we usually think of "orthodoxy" as meaning right teaching, the Greek word *doxa* also signifies praise; thus "orthodoxy" is also right praise.) For the Reformed tradition, the only true worship is the worship God has commanded, Scripture is the only source of revelation of God's will, and thus the right way of worshiping must be found in the Bible.[8]

Does Scripture, however, give any definite guidelines for worship? The early Calvinist Reformed theologians believed that it does. In the wider context of *pietas*, the first table of the law, a single verse served the Reformed tradition as a practical summary of the elements of corporate worship: Acts 2:42.

> And they continued steadfastly in the apostles' teaching and fellowship, in the breaking of bread and the prayers.[9]

Calvin's use of this verse in his *Institutes* reveals its paradigmatic character.

31

For as often as we partake of the symbol of the Lord's body, as a token given and received, we reciprocally bind ourselves to all the duties of love in order that none of us may permit anything that can harm our brother, or overlook anything that can help him, where necessity demands and ability suffices.

Luke relates in The Acts that this was the practice of the apostolic church, when he says that believers "continued in the apostles' teaching and fellowship, in the breaking of bread and in prayers" [Acts 2:42, cf. Vg.]. Thus it became the rule that no meeting of the church should take place without the Word, prayers, partaking of the Supper, and almsgiving.[10]

The meanings of the four elements of Acts 2:42 are explained in Calvin's commentary. First and most important is the teaching of the apostles, that is, the preaching of the gospel. This teaching is manifested visibly in the sacraments, represented here by the Lord's Supper. The gospel preaching also opens the way for the prayers (which include the praise and singing) of the church. The fellowship, *koinonia*, expressed biblically in the kiss of peace and especially in almsgiving, is the response to the gift of grace in Word and sacraments, a response which the Holy Spirit works in the hearts of believers.[11]

This description of the four key elements of proper Christian worship is particularly interesting for the way it includes *diakonia*, expressed in almsgiving, in the regular Sunday liturgy. Although the basis for this inclusion was biblical, it was also one response to a contemporary theological problem. Medieval Christians were very generous about charity, but long before the sixteenth century almsgiving had ceased to be a part of the order of the Mass, the proper worship service of the church. Protestants reintegrated charity into the chief liturgical event of Christian life, symbolically and practically drawing *leitourgia* and *diakonia* together again in the regular Sunday services. Almsgiving in worship, following the model of Acts 2:42, was both a symbolic and a practical bridge between Sunday and the rest of the week.[12]

It should be noted that this paradigm is a clear teaching of the Reformed church, not simply the explanation or interpretation of one isolated passage of the New Testament. In various ways the substance of this pattern for worship is found not only in comments scattered throughout John Calvin's works, but also in many other Reformed theologians of the sixteenth and seventeenth centuries. Unhappily, however, the normative status of Acts 2:42 gradually faded from theological consciousness, and this pattern for Reformed worship was forgotten. The fellowship-charity element was in fact the first thing to drop out, perhaps because people tended to divide the first table of the law (observance of the Sabbath: Word, sacraments, prayer) from the second table (care for the neighbor: alms).[13]

Nonetheless, in spite of the eclipse of Acts 2:42 as a theological paradigm, it is helpful to remember this classical Reformed understanding of worship and its pattern for relating *diakonia* with *leitourgia* in the regular Sunday service of the gathered Body of Christ. Almsgiving is not the only or even the chief form of *diakonia,* but its presence in the corporate worship of the church represents the close ties of *caritas* with *pietas,* of ministry to the neighbor with service to God. The rest of the week is visibly tied to the Sunday praise of God in the actual order of communal worship. This same liturgical order also emphasizes the fact that what we do from Monday through Saturday ought to flow out of our prayer life; it ought to be guided and nourished by hearing the Word preached and applied, and by sharing in the sacraments.

THE MINISTRY IN THE EARLY AND MEDIEVAL CHURCH WITH SPECIAL REGARD TO THE DIACONATE

If worship is the guide and nourishment for *diakonia,* it would seem logical that this should be evident not only in the order of Sunday worship but also in the leadership of the church, both on Sunday and throughout the week. What then is the role of the "ordained ministry" in relating *leitourgia* and *diakonia?* How are the ministers who lead the church in these services related to the rest of the church's members?

First, it is important to remember that the service of the church to God and the neighbor is the privilege and obligation of all Christians. It has, though, always been considered natural and right, and most would say biblical and necessary, to have specially chosen members of the community lead the rest in the public expression of ministry. In fact, the name "minister" (from the Latin equivalent of the Greek word *diakonos,* "servant") has—inappropriately—been restricted to those who hold the offices of leadership, although properly speaking all Christians are ministers: servants of God and of their neighbors. The principal difference between the congregation and the so-called ministers is the private or public character of their respective service. To avoid confusion, the word "minister" will here be used in its conventional sense of formal, public, ecclesiastical leadership. The proper meaning must be kept in mind, however, especially with regard to Protestant theology.[14]

The origin of the established public ministry of the Christian church is not at all clear. Modern scholars believe that the earliest Christian communities were not uniform in their organization; a variety of different, probably charismatic, leaders guided the scattered young churches. By the second century, one of these patterns, that of bishop, priest, and deacon, was beginning to spread, perhaps for reasons of practicality. It seems possible that the bishop-deacon (overseer-servant) pair developed in Hellenistic communities, paralleling the presbyter (ruler, priest) of Jewish tradition. At all events, when the three functions were gradually combined as established offices, the interrelationships among them, especially between presbyter-priest and deacon, were not clearly defined and remained a source of tension. Probably the early deacon was closely connected with the bishop (chief minister of a city) as the latter's assistant and subordinate, charged primarily with temporal and charitable matters, though also sharing certain liturgical responsibilities.

In the course of time, the functions of the diaconate began to change. Between the fourth and sixth centuries deacons lost most of their charitable role and acquired more and more liturgical duties. (This development may have been related to a shortage of priests, as floods of converts poured into the now legal church.) By the seventh century, deacons had become assistants to priests, as bishops became regional heads and the priestly role came to resemble that of an early bishop. Even though—or perhaps because—tensions between priests and deacons continued, the latter were fully integrated into a system of seven holy orders: bishop, priest, deacon, subdeacon, acolyte, lector, and doorkeeper.

The medieval understanding of the church's ministry, especially the diaconate, reflects the conception of the church's nature and of reality common at that time. Over the centuries the Hebraic sense of the value of the temporal had faded, and reality was increasingly seen as divided into a hierarchy of the sacred and the profane. This conception had significant implications for the understanding of the ecclesiastical status of leadership for *diakonia*. The place of the holy was identified with the church, with the ecclesiastical, while all the rest was worldly or profane. The church was the keeper of the means of grace, especially the sacraments, and these graces were distributed by the ordained clergy. Those in holy orders, whatever their personal behavior, had a special character because they were ordained to give the sacraments. In addition, because the temporal or worldly was understood as profane, those in holy orders were not supposed to be concerned with secular affairs, or at least the latter could never be their proper business.

It is probable that this theological conviction about the sacred and profane was one reason the diaconate was redefined as a liturgical office. At all events, by the later Middle Ages the church clearly taught that the deacon was an assistant to the priest, a man in training for the priesthood. The public ministry of the church was strictly "spiritual," carried out by specially chosen men who were necessary to mediate the grace of God to laypeople through the sacraments. The charitable functions of the church were not forgotten, but they were diffused among all Christians. For example, charitable collections were not a regular part of the liturgy of the Mass, though individual Christians gave generously to many kinds of causes. In one sense, this diffusion of responsibility for *diakonia* was entirely appropriate, but in practical fact it meant that the organization of *caritas* in the later Middle Ages was individualized, and the precise relationship between the needy and the church as a worshiping community, an institution, became rather unclear.

THE MINISTRY IN THE PROTESTANT REFORMATION

The teaching on the ministry is a part or subset of the doctrine of the church. That is, how the ordained ministry is explained is a function of how the church is defined. When Protestant reformers rejected the idea that the church is the necessary mediator of grace, the idea of the ministry also had to be redefined. Some things were clearly denied. No longer was the ordained ministry believed to be the only or necessary channel of grace. If we are justified by faith alone, access to salvation is by faith and not bound strictly to the sacramental system of the church and its special priesthood. If all Christians are by faith equal in the sight of God, there are no priests with special access to grace, and the ecclesiastical is not intrinsically more holy than the civil.

The revisioning of the doctrine of the church meant certain positive affirmations, the chief one being that justification by faith implies the priesthood of believers. In the priesthood of believers, each Christian is priest to all the sisters and brothers. This common priesthood does not mean individualism; indeed, the corporate nature of the church is reinforced by the fact that each person has the privilege and responsibility of intercession for all the others. If all believers are priests to each other because of their faith, then the religious and the ecclesiastical are not coterminous—that is, the visible structure of the church and its leadership are not all that is "religious."

What counted as a religious vocation was much more broadly defined for Protestants than for Roman Catholics, since Protestants no longer considered the secular (this-worldly) as profane. Any task done to glorify God and serve the neighbor was understood as a ministry. Furthermore, if the temporal could be as holy as the ecclesiastical, then lay Christians had as important a place in the church as did the clergy. Calvin's remarks on vocation in the *Institutes* are worth quoting.

> The Lord bids each one of us in all life's actions to look to his calling. . . . It is enough if we know that the Lord's calling is in everthing the beginning and foundation of well-doing. . . . No task will be so sordid and base, provided you obey your calling in it, that it will not shine and be reckoned very precious in God's sight.[15]

Even if all vocations can be religious and all Christians are ministers, however, not all these vocations are the public functions necessary for the church to be the church, not all these ministers have leadership roles.

Within the priesthood of believers, no individuals have a special holy character, but some individuals are called to fill particular offices. The ministry of the church belongs to all Christians, but some are chosen by God and the church to exercise publicly the duties which all carry out privately. Thus Protestants clearly denied any intrinsic difference between ordained and lay Christians, but they recognized important differences of office and function within the Body of Christ. Although Protestants rejected the idea of holy orders, they retained a very high view of the public ministry of the church because the latter is responsible for the preaching of the gospel; pastors are the contemporary voices of the sole recognized authority, the Bible. The calling to preach the Word, both orally and in the visible form of the sacraments of the Lord's Supper and baptism, was the highest office imaginable for Protestants.

Protestant agreement on the church as a priesthood of believers did not mean that all Protestants understood the church—or its public ministry—in identical fashion. For some Protestants, religious and civil communities were taken to be coterminous; the church and Christian society are, from an earthly point of view, identical. (This apparent coincidence of Christian and citizen does not mean all inhabitants of a territory are among the elect, but only that citizens and church members are the same people, and the earthly church is a mixture of wheat and chaff which only God can finally separate.) In this view, Christian rulers are the leading laity and thus the natural church members to hold the public offices of moral oversight, education, and relief for the poor. For example, among Lutherans and the Zwinglian Reformed, the ministry of Word and sacraments was the only clearly ecclesiastical office. Oversight of Christians' morals and care for their daily lives were happily left to the Christian prince or explicitly assigned to the Christian magistrate. Neither tradition made conscious provision for a situation in which the civil ruler was not Christian, an important factor for the development of *diakonia* in the post-Reformation age.

Certain Protestants, however, defined the church as a society distinct or distinguishable from the civil order. Radicals, who believed they could tell the difference between the wheat and the chaff, the elect and the reprobate, carried this idea to the extent of insisting that the church be separate from civil society. Calvinist Reformed, though they did not believe they could finally separate wheat and chaff, did teach that since the coming of Christ the church is theoretically distinguishable from the nation. For Calvinists, continuity between the Old Testament people of God and the New Testament people of God does not mean identical political organization for the church. In the Christian era, the civil and religious communities should be distinguishable in principle but ideally coterminous in practice. In effect, this view of Christian polity meant that all the ministries necessary for the church to be the church had to be distinct in theory from the offices of the civil society, but they did not have to be separate in fact in a Christian state when the ecclesiastical and civil societies coincided outwardly. Thus, among mainline Protestants, only Calvinists defined the church's ministry of *diakonia* as distinct and in theory separable from the charitable activity of the civil government, while at the same time acknowledging the civil welfare activities as Christian ministries.[16] In other words, the Calvinist understanding of the church's diaconate was unique in the sixteenth century because it was primarily ecclesiastical and able to exist in an autonomous church, and yet also able to accept and appreciate the possibility of cooperation with a civil welfare program in a context where the church was recognized or established by civil law.

AN OUTLINE OF THE CALVINIST REFORMED THEORY OF PLURAL MINISTRIES

What religious ministries did the Calvinist Reformed count as specifically ecclesiastical and necessary to the church's structure, whether or not it was a part of a Christian state?

The two fundamental and invariable offices of the church were the presbyter and the deacon, the representative leaders of worship and practical service. On the one hand, rejecting the traditional idea that bishop *(episkopos)* and priest *(presbyteros)* in the New Testament refer to different orders, Reformed theologians insisted that these and other names, such as "pastor" and "minister," refer to one ecclesiastical rank or office of ministry of Word and sacraments (and government).[17] On the other hand, care for spiritual needs by presbyters and care for temporal needs by deacons, leadership in worship or leadership in service of the neighbor, are different roles. Presbyters and deacons require certain gifts in common, but the two functions also require some gifts which differ. One person may conceivably be fitted to fill either office, but normally both tasks together are too much for a single individual. The functions of the presbyter are primary, as the proclamation of God's forgiveness and justifying grace comes before the birth of new life and service to the poor. It is clear, however, that love of the neighbor is the most unmistakable evidence of our love for God, so it is essential that the church have a diaconal office and not leave this religious duty only to individual Christians or the civil authority.

The office of the presbyter, the chief ecclesiastical ministry, includes a number of tasks. The principal one recognized by all Protestants was preaching the Word and administering the sacraments. The second and third, claimed by the Calvinist Reformed, were teaching and moral guidance or discipline. All three of these functions are the responsibility of the pastoral office; other presbyters, however, take part in the second and third tasks.

The second presbyterial office of the Calvinist Reformed church was charged with teaching the faith and defending the purity of doctrine. This function was the one least easily distinguished from that of the pastor and thus usually the most difficult to maintain as a separate office. The equivalent today might be professors of theology, catechists, Sunday school teachers, parents, and others who train church members in the understanding of their faith.[18]

The elders of the Calvinist Reformed church were "lay" ecclesiastical leaders elected to work with the pastor in overseeing the daily lives of the congregation, helping resolve conflicts, counseling, admonishing, and (if finally necessary) disciplining those whose lives or beliefs required rebuke. The office of elder was in fact the focus of the most intense controversy in the sixteenth century. This dispute was not primarily because people disliked discipline, although that was an important element of the social objections. The chief difficulty was the battle between ecclesiastical and civil authorities for the control of discipline. No one denied the need for or appropriateness of moral guidance and oversight, but princes and magistrates did not wish to leave such powers in the hands of ecclesiastical authorities, while Calvinist Reformed theologians insisted that counseling and correction are necessary functions of the church's ministry which cannot simply be delegated to the state.[19]

In addition to reconceiving the presbyterial ministry, Calvinist Reformed also redefined the office of deacon. No longer were deacons liturgical assistants to priests; their office was an ecclesiastical ministry of care for the poor and unfortunate, an office which should be permanent in the church. (This teaching will be examined more closely in chapter four.) Thus the fully developed doctrine of plural ministries among Calvinist Reformed included four offices: the pastor, the teacher, the elder, and the deacon.

From where did the Calvinist Reformed get their idea of

the necessary ministries of the church? The key source, and certainly the one explicitly claimed by Martin Bucer, John Calvin, and others, was Scripture. The *fundamental,* though often implicit, basis for the conception of ecclesiastical ministry as plural was obviously the Calvinist Reformed understanding of the third use of the law, the parallel duties of worship *(pietas)* and love *(caritas)* as inseparable. Combined with this basic theological stance was the conviction that the New Testament has certain differences from the Old, specifically a different way of relating civil and ecclesiastical authorities so that the society of the church is theoretically distinguishable from society in general. Thus those responsible for charity were necessarily distinguishable in theory from civil officers in charge of relief for the poor.

These general, biblically based convictions were not all that Calvinist Reformed had as foundations for a plurality of ministries. More explicit in the reformers' writings was the view that Scripture, which is authoritative not only for doctrine but also for polity and worship, indicates that there were a variety of offices in the New Testament. Here it must be remembered that sixteenth-century exegetes, even those like Calvin who were not rigid literalists, did not understand the variety of offices in the New Testament the way modern scholars do. When twentieth-century writers speak of the differences among early Christian churches, they mean that there was no uniform organization for the scattered communities. When Calvin and other pre-Enlightenment exegetes spoke of diverse offices in the New Testament, they meant that each church had several kinds of leaders but these several were essentially the same in all the communities.

For premodern exegetes the Bible was a whole, God's revelation to human beings, but it was as obvious to them as to us that individually the writings which tell us of the early church are incomplete pictures. Different books have various names for gifts and leaders. According to Calvinist Reformed theologians, these various ministries must be coordinated in order for the contemporary church to model itself on God's will as found in Scripture. Besides the challenge of fitting different Scripture passages together, theologians also faced the problem of determining which offices of the early church were applicable to all ages. This second difficulty was harder to resolve, but a study of the functions of the various New Testament ministries and the differences between a new movement and an established institution served to guide Calvin and others in distinguishing permanent from temporary ministries.

Each of the four permanent ecclesiastical ministries was established or supported by biblical texts, as was the theory of plural ministries itself. The texts on which the largely unquestioned pastoral office was based are too numerous to name, although Ephesians 4:11 and 1 Corinthians 12:28 and many in the epistles to Timothy and Titus are noteworthy. Those supporting a separate teaching ministry were Ephesians 4:11 and 1 Corinthians 12:28; those distinguishing a separate office of discipline were 1 Corinthians 12:28, Romans 12:8, and 1 Timothy 5:17. The biblical bases for the Reformed diaconate were Acts 6:1-6, 1 Timothy 3:8-13 and 5:3-10, and Romans 12:8 and 16:1-2, with the possible addition of 1 Corinthians 12:28. These lists obviously overlap a great deal, and the texts mentioned several times are in fact the verses which support the plurality of ministries. Ephesians 4:11 is the first:

> And he gave some to be apostles; and some, prophets; and some evangelists; and some, pastors and doctors.[20]

Then follows 1 Corinthians 12:28:

> And God hath set some in the church, first apostles, secondly prophets, thirdly teachers, then miracles, then gifts of healings, helps, governments, divers kinds of tongues.[21]

Finally, there is Romans 12:8:

> Let us give ourselves to our ministry; . . . he that exhorteth, to his exhorting; he that giveth, let him do it with liberality; he that ruleth, with diligence; he that sheweth mercy, with cheerfulness.[22]

The Calvinist Reformed tradition, beginning with Martin Bucer, noted clearly the overlapping in these texts and made an effort to understand how these Pauline lists fitted together and which offices were intended to be permanent in church order. Since John Calvin's discussion of the doctrine of the ministry is the most orderly, consistent, and influential, his treatment of the teaching is used as the focus here.

The three series of names given in Ephesians 4:11, 1 Corinthians 12:28, and Romans 12:8 seem to be varieties of gifts of the Holy Spirit more than specific offices. However, Christian theologians have never fully agreed on distinctions among charisms, duties, and structured offices. Calvin recognized that these lists name gifts, but he believed that gifts and offices go together. In his comment on Ephesians 4:11 he explains.

> Now, we might be surprised that, when he is speaking of the gifts of the Holy Spirit, Paul should enumerate offices instead of gifts. I reply, whenever men are called by God, gifts are necessarily connected with offices. For God does not cover men with a mask in appointing them apostles or pastors, but also furnishes them with gifts, without which they cannot properly discharge their office.[23]

Granting that gifts and offices are the same in these New Testament lists, and the number of offices is reduced when the overlap in the verses is recognized, there still remain more offices than the Calvinist four. How did Reformed theologians account for this discrepancy?

Believing that Scripture provides a model for the ministry of the church did not mean that Calvin felt the pattern was intended to be transferred in every detail from one age to another. Like other theologians, the Genevan Reformer appreciated the difference between the initiation of a movement and its organized institutional form. He explicitly distinguished between the offices necessary for establishing (or reforming) the church,[24] and those required for its ordinary ongoing life.

Those who preside over the government of the church in accordance with Christ's institution are called by Paul as follows: first apostles, then prophets, thirdly evangelists, fourthly pastors, and finally teachers [Eph. 4:11]. Of these only the last two have an ordinary office in the church; the Lord raised up the first three at the beginning of his Kingdom, and now and again revives them as the need of the times demands. . . .

Here it must now be noted that to this point we have considered only those offices which are engaged in the ministry of the Word; nor does Paul mention the others in the fourth chapter of the letter to the Ephesians, which we have cited [Eph. 4:11]. But in the letter to the Romans [Rom. 12:7-8] and in the first letter to the Corinthians [1 Cor. 12:28], he lists others, as powers, the gift of healing, interpretation, government, and caring for the poor. Two of these I omit as being temporary, for it is not worthwhile to tarry over them. But two of them are permanent: government and caring for the poor.[25]

These quotations show how Calvin reasoned in developing a fourfold ministry. He combined a strong sense of history that seems almost modern with a typical pre-Enlightenment conviction that a unified picture of New Testament church order could be found. To this picture he added the characteristic Reformed belief that the contemporary church must practice this apostolic pattern. The result was a teaching on a biblically based plurality of offices considered permanently necessary in every age for the church to be the church.

CRITIQUE OF CALVIN'S TEACHING ON THE MINISTRY

A number of scholars have questioned how much of this Reformed ecclesiastical structure is really biblical. For example, some object to the distinction between temporal and permanent offices, although the influential *Baptism, Eucharist and Ministry* document of the Faith and Order commission does not seem to find this distinction quite such a problem, at least as a general principle. Some attribute the Calvinist theory of a double diaconate of separate administrators and nurses to social influence. (This argument will be considered at the end of chapter three.) Other critics point to political and theological motives contributing to the development of the office of elder.[26]

Often the questions focus on the details of Calvin's biblical grounds for his doctrine of the ministry, and here there is place for legitimate criticism. A number of conscious and unconscious influences were undoubtedly at work in the minds of the teachers and pastors who developed the Reformed doctrine of the plural ministry. Some of these may be more clear to us than to them, others we may in fact misinterpret. (It is useful to bear in mind that some of what appears ill founded to us may have explanations we do not see.)

Another way of evaluating Calvin's teaching on the ministry, especially its plural character of presbyter and deacon, however, sets the doctrine in the wider context of biblical theology, and here the Reformed teaching stands firm. Although less easy to prove, this approach is particularly interesting in terms of the diaconate and the usefulness of sixteenth-century teaching for the twentieth century. We may find that our age is not as different from Calvin's as we think.

It is clear that no one in the sixteenth century denied that both worship and service are the responsibility of all Christians. In addition, everyone agreed that the first of these tasks should be the responsibility of chosen leaders of the church. The question was whether the second part, *diakonia*, should also have a specific place or leadership in the visible structure of the church. An affirmative answer would imply a plurality of ministries: presbyterial and diaconal.

Different religious traditions gave different answers to the question of a visible ecclesiastical structure for *diakonia*. Some Christians did not make deacons of poor relief an office at all. For example, Roman Catholics kept the name "deacon" for a liturgical minister but diffused the function of *diakonia* among all Christians, not assigning social concerns to any specific office. Almost all Protestants did provide structures for charitable activity, each having certain characteristic strengths and weaknesses. Lutherans and Zwinglians established structures for *diakonia* in the Christian community but assigned this diaconal office to the Christian civil authorities as the leading laity. Eventually, these welfare functions were no longer understood as ecclesiastical but simply as civil. Radicals, whose communities wished to be completely separate from civil society, often established diaconates for themselves but made no place for a relationship with social welfare institutions of the larger society.

The Calvinist Reformed interpretation of the church as in but not of the world led to the theory of an ecclesiastical ministry of *diakonia* which could overlap with the welfare program of a civil government. This primarily ecclesiastical diaconal structure which could still cooperate with civil welfare organizations presented certain practical difficulties. Nonetheless, because it can in theory function in a situation of separation of church and state but still cooperate with nonecclesiastical organizations for human welfare, the Calvinist Reformed understanding of the church's diaconal ministry seems to offer one of the best patterns for relating corporate ethics to corporate worship in the religiously plural global village of the modern world.

Chapter Three

THE SOCIAL CONTEXT

The service which Christians, individually or corporately, offer to their neighbours springs from their relationship and obedience to Jesus Christ as Lord. But its form at any particular time and place depends on the nature of the neighbourhood. Whenever organized service fails to take seriously and adjust freely to its environment it becomes barren and irrelevant.

A. A. Brash, "The Church's Diakonia"[1]

DIAKONIA IS THE church's service to the world, or, as some modern Christians would say, the church's service in the world. To understand the Reformed diaconate rightly, therefore, one must examine the social context in which the reformers worked. This context has clear elements of both continuity and discontinuity with the past and the future. Some of the theological continuities and discontinuities have been seen above. This chapter considers the economic and social situation along with the changes in welfare that the sixteenth century found necessary. In some ways, the sixteenth and twentieth centuries have much in common.

Many twentieth-century Christians in the West today live

in a world which is very confused about responsibility for social programs. Separation of church and state contributes to the ambiguity of the problem, but in fact perplexity and conflict over the relationship between civil and ecclesiastical authorities in the care for the unfortunate has a long history. It may be of use to contemporary students of the question to examine the early modern world for the roots of the present situation.

The sixteenth century is known as the age of great intellectual and religious changes, but it was also a time of social transformation. One of the major social changes was in the area of welfare. In fact, the sixteenth century is often seen as the beginning of modern social welfare. The widespread reorganization of benevolence in this period was not simply the result of a desire for innovation. As with the simultaneous Renaissance and Reformation movements, the reform of relief for the poor was a response to a situation for which traditional solutions seemed inadequate and sometimes even wrong.

MEDIEVAL CHARITABLE PRACTICES

Traditionally, charitable activity in general and the care of the poor in particular had been the province of the ecclesiastical authorities. Charity has always been understood as an extremely important religious duty of all Christians, and generous almsgiving was a highly honored virtue in the Middle Ages. A variety of religious organizations existed wholly or in part for a broad range of benevolent purposes. Some institutions, such as monasteries, provided a limited amount of charity, although this concern was subordinate to the primary work of prayer for the saving of the world and the monks' own souls. Bishops and local parish priests were supposed to assist any poor who came to their attention.[2]

In the later Middle Ages, the ways charity was distributed became increasingly diverse and individualized. Nobles or other wealthy individuals or groups often established foundations to pray for their souls and to assist poor and needy Christians. Sometimes these foundations were actual almshouses (called "hospitals," although they had no real medical function), sometimes they were donations of food or other gifts on certain occasions. Special collections were frequently made to care for lepers and other sick, and to support homes for orphans, travelers, and many other kinds of needy folk. Collections were also made for the building and repairing of churches and sometimes roads or bridges, or for the support or decoration of shrines or reliquaries, because the religious duty of charity included all forms of ecclesiastically approved giving. (A modern parallel is found in today's secular governments which recognize as tax deductible a wide variety of charities, including schools, community improvement organizations, and so forth.)

The most pervasive form of charity was probably the simple distribution of alms to local or wandering beggars. Since poverty was a virtue, religious people sometimes renounced their possessions and became beggars, adding to the number of poor for whom there was no other choice than appeal to Christian charity.

THE SITUATION IN 1500

In the late Middle Ages the organization of ecclesiastical charity began to encounter increasing difficulties.[3] Over time lay Christians had come to take an ever more active role in organizing and managing benevolence. At first this development meant more foundations by wealthy individuals and confraternities, as the number of nonnoble patrons grew with the development of urban power and initiative. In time, as the merchant classes became impatient with the fiscal ineptitude of clerical administrators, lay Christians took a larger part in running as well as endowing charitable institutions.

Special impetus was given to the gradual cultural changes in benevolence because by the fourteenth and fifteenth centuries traditional solutions were proving inadequate to deal with Christendom's poor. A variety of ills, from famine and the waves of bubonic plague which washed over Europe to the ravages of the Hundred Years War, expanded the dimensions of the problem. To traditional categories of beggars, such as orphans, chronic invalids, uprooted serfs, and those like the Franciscan and Dominican friars who renounced ownership for religious reasons, now were added the wandering (mercenary) soldiers loosed on the countryside after discharge from the intermittent wars. Certain fiscal and other abuses, combined with a lack of imagination, limited the response of ecclesiastical authorities to the problem of relief for the poor, and gradually lay leadership moved toward civil control of charitable institutions. Since the problem was most urgent in urban areas, the cities became the pioneers in social welfare reform.

CHANGES IN CHARITABLE PRACTICES IN THE SIXTEENTH CENTURY

The reform of social welfare in the sixteenth century brought about a number of practical changes which began to reshape charitable practices in ways familiar to modern eyes.[4] Some of the most widespread changes were organizational, involving the centralization, laicization, and rationalization of benevolence in Western Europe. In great measure these were practical alterations which aimed to systematize charity under more efficient leadership. "Centralization" means that usually the many scattered charitable foundations were more or less expeditiously consolidated into one or sometimes several purses or common chests. Often one convenient "hospital" was also retained as a general administrative center and home for the poor who needed institutional care.

"Laicization" signifies that the administration of the common chest was usually overseen by the civil authorities. Not only were the administrators laypeople, but they were also responsible to the civil more than, or even in place of, the ecclesiastical authorities. Although the spiritual needs of the poor continued to be the concern of the clergy, the clergy normally had little real influence in the actual running of these institutions. The lay alms officers were ordinarily chosen from among the important citizens of a city. Sometimes the same individuals handled finances and the daily distribution of aid. In some places, however, these duties were divided between the committee which took care of the funds and audited the books, and a single full-time administrator who handled the day-to-day affairs of the central hospital and provided aid to the noninstitutionalized poor.

Reordering welfare to make it more efficient meant not only centralized funds and better trained businessmen to administer the money, but also a more rational organization of the details of charitable activity. New regulations were established for determining who qualified for charitable assistance. The civil officers who administered the program first investigated the particular needs of the poor. They then made lists of those who required aid and noted both the kind and degree of assistance necessary. Distinctions were made between institutionalized indigent and others, between local and foreign unfortunates, and sometimes between temporary and permanent kinds of needs. Some poor (for example, orphans, or those with special kinds of diseases) might require institutional care; others could be helped in their homes by weekly doles, for which sometimes special tokens or certificates were issued. Some unfortunates needed only temporary assistance because of illness or business reversals, and these were often aided secretly to save them shame. Others were public charges for years, although in the case of orphans apprenticeships and dowries were arranged so that the children might become self-sufficient members of society. Earlier tendencies to give priority to local needy were strengthened. Most civil ordinances provided for those among their own people who could not support themselves, but they refused or greatly restricted the aid available for foreigners.

One of the key problems faced by the new civil administrators was that of the hordes of wandering beggars. Solutions to this difficulty were generally similar; most authorities did their best to control or limit or even eliminate begging. Distinctions were frequently made between the invalid and healthy beggars, and often work was found for the latter. Sometimes new industries were even established to create employment.

ARGUMENTS ON SOCIAL WELFARE REFORM

It is evident from the above why the reform of charity in the sixteenth century is often seen as the beginning of modern social welfare. There are some controversies among historians regarding what exactly was new about the sixteenth-century movement.[5] Most of these issues can be sketched fairly quickly. No one questions that, although precedents existed, centralization and rationalization were new as widespread practices. Historians disagree to some extent whether laicization was really new; the process had been going on for a considerable time, though Protestant teaching on the priesthood of believers supplied new justification for it. The idea that each locality is obligated to care for its own poor, the question of taxation for relief of the poor, and the distinguishing of invalid and healthy beggars are all debated, but these seem to be refinements of tradition, or civil rules derived from canon (ecclesiastical) law. Perhaps what is new is not one detail or another but the combination of all and the sheer extent of the reform.

One of the most interesting and possibly most significant of the "new" features of sixteenth-century welfare reform is the question of the restraint of begging, the solution to one of the alms administrators' chief difficulties. Some scholars suggest that this apparent change, like several of the others, is simply the extention of existing practices. Others maintain that, at least in principle and in most places in fact, the prohibition of begging was a new departure. The restrictions on begging were not identical everywhere. In Roman Catholic areas licensed begging was permitted because poverty and almsgiving were understood as meritorious, a means to salvation. In Protestant areas begging was totally forbidden; Martin Luther's words express the common Protestant position.

> Probably one of our greatest needs is to abolish all mendicancy everywhere in Christendom. No one living among Christians ought to go begging. It would be an easy law to make, if only we dared, and were in earnest that every town should support its own poor.[6]

Where neither poverty nor charity in itself can earn salvation, and one glorifies God by any honest work, healthy beggars are regarded as lazy. But those who cannot work should be supported without the shame and temptation to deceit of begging.

The question of begging leads naturally to consideration of the arguments on the means and the motives for charitable giving. Indeed, some of these questions continue to puzzle modern Christians. For example, is there a distinction between caring for the church building or paying the pastor, and giving for charity? Should all gifts be lumped together? One problem created by centralization of funds was the possible diversion of benevolence from the poor to other charitable objects such as the support of church or school. Sometimes such diversions happened, but often separate purses (budgets) were established for the various sorts of needs, just as modern Reformed churches often separate ordinary expenses from benevolence giving. Should the state intervene to see that charitable funds are collected? On certain occasions Roman Catholic as well as Protestant rulers ordered compulsory contributions (taxes) for relief of the poor, but this was rare; support for benevolence projects continued to be drawn chiefly from endowment and current gifts.

But why had people established charitable foundations in the first place? Why did they continue to give? One of the traditional purposes of charitable activity was the salvation of the soul, both the souls of the givers and those of the recipients who were moved to pray for their benefactors. This practice was discriminating in the sense that it was done to serve a definite end, and the poverty of the recipients constituted their worthiness.

For Protestants, although charity is the natural outpouring of justification, almsgiving could not contribute to anyone's salvation. Although they believed in bearing their problems patiently, Protestants desacralized poverty. Being poor is not a virtue in itself but simply one state of human existence among others. Work is a necessary expression of service to God and the neighbor, unless one cannot work. Poverty itself was not, however, considered sinful; it was seen as a problem which Christians should try to mitigate for any who could not help themselves. From this Protestant viewpoint, Roman Catholic almsgiving to healthy beggars who could work seemed indiscriminate; it was not charity but irresponsible stewardship. The new valuation of work—not as a means of earning or even proving salvation but as an expression of gratitude and responsible use of God-given talents—was clearly a critical factor in the prohibition of begging among Protestants.

To sixteenth-century Roman Catholics, as to some modern observers, however, the Protestant doctrine of justification by faith alone seemed to cut the nerve of any desire to do good or to be generous. This reasoning may indeed have affected some people, but no one who really understood the meaning of justifying grace would stop helping the poor and needy. Remember Martin Luther's formula, "The Christian is a perfectly free lord of all, . . . the Christian is a perfectly dutiful servant of all." Thus, the new Christian liberty often led to great generosity. Christians who recognized themselves as freed from having to work for their salvation served their neighbors to honor and thank God for their salvation. Justification by faith may also have made some people more generous, since it was easier to believe that the smallness of a poor person's gift did not affect the giver's salvation.

Who was reponsible for the changes in social welfare? Here we find the most heated arguments regarding the reform of social welfare in the sixteenth century. It is generally agreed that the new patterns of relief for the poor were first fully organized and implemented in the cities of South Germany; the ordinance of Nuremberg in 1522 is apparently the first to include all the main features. The ideas soon spread across Western Europe, through Roman Catholic as well as Protestant lands. Who then, if anyone, can claim credit for the reform of welfare? Was it Lutheran, humanist, or (medieval) Roman Catholic in origin? Most scholars concede that the social reformers who drafted the first ordinance of Nuremberg were Lutheran, but can the social changes be attributed to their

Lutheranism? Even if some early social reformers were Lutheran, many writers say that being Protestant was not necessary for the establishment of the reforms themselves. Some of these scholars believe that the welfare reforms were simply a development of medieval Roman Catholic practices, while others argue that much of what is new is the work of Christian humanists, both Catholic and Protestant.

Who deserves the credit for the social reforms may be a *question mal posée*, unanswerable because of the way it is phrased. If the basic idea is reworded as a question of the relationship(s) between the social reforms and the other movements of the sixteenth century, however, some interesting observations are possible. What was the relationship of the social welfare reforms to the various Reformations? It is probable that theology did affect some of the ways the social reform was understood and implemented. The different regulations for the restraint of begging are perhaps the clearest practical example of this influence. Apart from that issue, however, the organization of the new social welfare system was similar across confessional lines. The justification for the new system was clearly not always the same. In some ways the most interesting feature of the social reform is not the organization of practical details but the way the practice is fitted into different religious worldviews.

How did each of the major religious communities come to terms with the social welfare reforms? For those on each end of the theological spectrum, the welfare reforms remained something of a difficulty. The clearest case is that of the Radicals, for whom charity was the responsibility of the church, not the state. The civil system was a part of the unregenerate world and therefore basically ignored. For Roman Catholics, charity was ecclesiastical in much the same way as for Radicals, except that the state was accepted as Christian and seen as subordinate to the church. In the sixteenth century, Roman Catholic princes were usurping traditional episcopal control of charitable institutions and leaving insignificant or sometimes only token roles for the clergy. This development had the potential to produce a tension between theology (ecclesiastical control) and practice (civil control), even though princes and bishops usually got along amicably in fact.

Most Protestants approved of the civil social welfare reform because they understood it as a function of the priesthood of believers, of lay leadership in the church. According to Lutherans and Zwinglians, it was suitable or even right that the Christian ruler(s) should have charge of benevolence, so the integration of the social reforms into the religious view was complete. Calvinist Reformed were plainly Protestant in their affirmation of lay leadership in welfare, but they insisted that these lay offices of relief for the poor are primarily ecclesiastical, and only secondarily, though also appropriately, civil. This curious Calvinist both/and (ecclesiastical and civil) attitude toward the welfare reforms can be better explained in connection with an examination of the social practices of sixteenth-century Geneva.

THE GENEVAN SITUATION AND ARGUMENTS RELATING WELFARE REFORM TO CALVIN'S DIACONATE

How did the charitable situation in Geneva fit into the social welfare reform movement of the sixteenth century? How was John Calvin's teaching related to the institutions in his city established to help the poor?

The answer to the first question has two parts, which in legal language might be called the "established" and the "disestablished" forms of the diaconate. The established diaconate in Geneva was very similar to social welfare developments elsewhere in Europe, but a brief sketch here may be useful.

Geneva was a small city-state on a crossroads for trade among French-, Italian-, and German-speaking territories of Western Europe. In the 1530s Geneva rejected its prince bishop and declared itself Protestant. As part of the new municipal organization, the city centralized benevolence and replaced the disjointed medieval charitable foundations with a new General

Hospital in 1535.[7] The old endowments (often consisting of rents from farmlands) were combined. However, since much of Geneva's countryside had been lost to the neighboring states of Savoy or Bern as the price of the city's struggle to become Protestant, the worth of the foundations was somewhat reduced. The government took on the responsibility of collecting the monies owed to the Hospital, and as these funds sometimes were mixed with the rest of the civil budget, the government became the major support of the charitable system. Taxation was never instituted, but voluntary contributions were encouraged and begging was strictly prohibited.

Several kinds of administrators were chosen. Civil officers, known as "procurators," were elected to manage and allocate the finances. A single administrator, called a "hospitaller," settled in the convent left by the nuns of St. Clare, where he, his wife, and a number of servants cared for the institutionalized poor and distributed aid to the needy who remained in their homes. Calvin was not directly involved in the running of the city welfare system, although as pastor and concerned city resident he complained to the authorities about this system, as he did about other aspects of life, when he believed things were not being handled responsibly.

The disestablished form of the diaconate in Geneva was a parallel voluntary organization set up by groups of refugees to do for their needy what the city poor-relief system did for Genevan citizens. The earliest and best known of the refugee charitable purses was called the "French Fund," the *Bourse française*.[8] This was a central fund or account organized by French-speaking refugees and administered by those they elected. (Calvin was a strong supporter of and frequent contributor to this fund.) The refugees divided the duties of their diaconal personnel slightly differently than did the civil poor-relief system. The collectors and auditors handled most of the administrative business, though some of the latter was done by the deacons who had the individual care of the needy. Nonetheless, both the established or civil welfare system and the disestablished or voluntary organization of noncitizens carried out the Reformed diaconal tasks of administering the money given to support those in distress and of caring for the poor personally.

The question of the relationship of Calvin's diaconate to the charitable activities in Geneva is a rather difficult one, and not all agree on the answer. Social historians have compared the development of Calvin's teaching on the diaconate with the welfare reform movement and concluded that the Reformer basically copied or adopted the civil system.[9] The argument goes as follows. The city welfare system was established in 1535, the year before Calvin came. The Reformer maintained that his diaconate was based on scriptural exegesis, but partway through his time in Geneva he developed a double diaconate which has marked similarities to the dual personnel of the civil welfare organization. The Reformer's reasons for doing such a thing are not usually discussed at length. Some suggest that making the civil officers deacons was a way to consecrate the civil organization in order to enhance its value in the eyes of both administrators and people. Recognition as an ecclesiastical ministry would also perhaps permit some real clerical influence if not control.

In considering this social-influence theory of Calvin's diaconate, one must distinguish several questions. The first is whether Calvin simply established a diaconate by consecrating the welfare reforms. A negative answer to this question seems plain in view of the theological context of *diakonia* and the doctrine of the church, discussed in the previous chapter. That a diaconate as such was not developed because of the social reforms is obvious when one considers the weight Calvin gave to the pairing of the two tables of the law, *pietas* and *caritas*, and the common Protestant effort to renew a Christian office of charity. That Calvin had every reason to approve of lay, secular leadership of the religious task of charity is clear when his view of the priesthood of believers and lay leadership is remembered. Recognizing the role of Christian laity in relief for the poor was consistent with all Protestant teaching; it was not a question of political expediency. That the office of deacon was (primarily) ecclesiastically based is apparent in

Calvin's active support for a disestablished diaconate, which illustrates his view that religious and civil societies can (as well as should) be distinguishable. Thus a lay ecclesiastical diaconate is possible without a civil base, and the social reform movement cannot be said to have caused Calvin to develop a distinct office for the relief of the poor as a necessary ministry of the church.

Another question raised by the social historians is the matter of the shape of Calvin's ecclesiastical office of charity, and this criticism appears much better grounded. Though the diaconate itself is clearly a theologically based teaching, which can function in established or disestablished form, what about social influence as a cause for a double diaconate? Even if the Calvinist Reformed doctrine of ecclesiastical-civil relationships could accommodate a both/and approach to the way deacons and social workers are related, was the practice of a twofold diaconate copied from the civil order? Logically it does look as if Calvin followed the Genevan practice in organizing two kinds of deacons, and there is good evidence for the social-influence theory. Certainly the practical efficiency of the civil poor-relief system must have appealed to Calvin, as it obviously did to other Protestants. A division of labor in the care of the poor and sick would have seemed very orderly to Calvin the Christian and Calvin the humanist. Social influence as a source of a double diaconate cannot, though, tell the whole story and may possibly distort the picture slightly. A different, theological solution to this problem is offered in the next chapter, in the discussion of the Scripture texts to which Calvin appealed in defining his doctrine of the diaconate.

Social influences on theological teaching are certainly not wrong; the expression of Christian faith, especially *diakonia,* must take into account the world that the church is called to serve. Thus it is right and natural to ask how the social welfare reform of the sixteenth century (the historical context), as well as the doctrine of the church (the theological context), contributed to shaping the Reformed teaching on the diaconate. What still needs to be added, however, is an investigation of the theological definition of the Calvinist Reformed diaconate and how that teaching was related to the one critical source of religious authority, the Bible.

Chapter Four

THE CLASSICAL REFORMED DIACONATE

It is important to bear in mind that Luther's teaching on diakonia was the sequel of a precise theological reformation and not a mere reformation of Church order or discipline or social practice.

J. Atkinson, "Diakonia at the Time of the Reformation"

Since I undertook the office of teacher in the church, I have had no other purpose than to benefit the church by maintaining the pure doctrine of godliness. . . .
Moreover, it has been my purpose in this labor to prepare and instruct candidates in sacred theology for the reading of the divine Word, in order that they may be able both to have easy access to it and to advance in it without stumbling.

J. Calvin, "To the Reader," *Institutes of the Christian Religion*[1]

FOR JOHN CALVIN as well as for Martin Luther, theology was the fundamental source and shaper of the teaching on *diakonia*. This was not just any theology, however; the whole intent of Calvin's work was to proclaim and teach the Word of God pure-

61

ly, and this was as true for the question of the diaconate as for all the other doctrines. Calvin certainly was not the only Reformed theologian concerned with the church's ministry to the world. His older colleague and mentor Martin Bucer is sometimes called the theologian of *diakonia*,[2] and Calvin learned a great deal from the Reformer of Strasbourg. However, the Genevan Reformer's teaching on the diaconate both developed the doctrine and expressed it more coherently and lucidly, and his formulation became dominant in Calvinism. Thus Calvin's diaconate serves as the paradigmatic example of the classical Reformed teaching on this subject.

Before turning to a full discussion of the Calvinist Reformed diaconate, however, it is useful to clarify how the term "deacon" was used in the sixteenth century.

DEFINITIONS OF "DEACON" IN THE SIXTEENTH CENTURY

The office of the deacon suffered from confusion as much in the sixteenth century as it has in the twentieth. As seen earlier, the traditional deacon of the late Middle Ages was a liturgical assistant to the priest. The diaconate had lost its intrinsic identity and become largely a stage on the ladder to the priesthood. Protestants reacted sharply against this idea. For one thing, they rejected the biblical interpretation on which the liturgical diaconate was based, as will be seen below. For another, most Protestants considered the service of the poor and sick a function which required its own distinct place and specific leadership. All of the faithful should care for their neighbors, but the church should also give specific leadership to this common Christian duty. The traditional arrangement, which added charitable responsibilities to the work of the minister of Word and sacraments, was generally rejected. Because Protestants affirmed that the civil realm has a God-given integrity of its own, they did not expect or wish pastors alone to handle all the church's business. Certainly the poor must be aided, but ministers of the Word should not be distracted from preaching by the management of church property, as medieval bishops had been.

The diaconal situation and language of the sixteenth century can be summed up in the following way. Roman Catholic deacons were auxiliary liturgical ministers, third in rank of those ordained to holy orders, and usually promoted to the priesthood after a period as liturgical assistant. Care of the poor had no specific ecclesiastical head, although charity was considered the responsibility of every Christian, especially of bishops. German-speaking Protestants, especially Zwinglian Reformed, continued to use the name "deacon" for assistant pastors, but they clearly assigned the care of the needy to civil alms officers, understood as lay leaders—lay bishops—in the Christian community. Sometimes the name "deacon" could also be used for these civil administrators of welfare. Some Anabaptist communities, for example, the Hutterites, established "deacons of material needs" as parallels to their "deacons of the Word."[3] Of course, Anabaptists would have nothing to do with the civil poor-relief system.

Calvinist Reformed almost without exception retained the name "deacon" for an ecclesiastical minister, but they redefined the duties of the office in Protestant style as care of the poor. The civil alms officers were recognized as in fact deacons of the church, with a certain responsibility to the civil authority but primary status as ecclesiastical ministers. As was seen in the previous chapter, however, the Calvinist Reformed diaconate could also function in a disestablished fashion, because its primary foundation was ecclesiastical. Thus, ecclesiastical deacons did not have to be civil welfare officers, and they could exist under any civil authority. Either way, whether legally established (as was proper in a Christian society), or possessing no civil status (as would be true for refugees or those under a hostile government), Calvinist deacons were understood theologically as ecclesiastical ministers of benevolence. They were unique among sixteenth-century deacons or welfare ministers, however, because they could exist with equal integrity alone or in cooperation with a civil system.

AN OUTLINE OF CALVIN'S TEACHING
ON THE DIACONATE

Most simply put, John Calvin's teaching on the diaconate defined it as a permanent ecclesiastical ministry of care for the poor and sick, the ministry of the church as a body to the physical suffering of human beings.[4]

The fully developed doctrine can be sketched in the following way. The diaconate is understood as the fourth kind of ecclesiastical ministry, after the three presbyterial offices of pastor, teacher, and elder. As *office* it is necessary and permanent, although a single individual may not remain an active deacon for life. Deacons are not servants or deputies of the presbyters, as were those procurators employed by medieval bishops to care for temporal business. Deacons are, however, second to presbyters in rank, because the first table of the law (worship), takes precedence over the second (love). The diaconate is a ministry of the church, established to care for the poor and sick because the church corporately (as well as individually) has a responsibility for the mundane service of Christ's sisters and brothers who are suffering most. Calvin understood the diaconate to have two major functions, the collection and administration of finances, and the actual, physical, personal care for the needy. These tasks he divided between two sorts of personnel, administrators and nurses, or men and women. The men were dominant and were the only ones who should be ordained. The women were supposed to be elderly widows who, because they were themselves often destitute, both served the church and were supported by it.

Calvin's teaching on the diaconate is expressed most succinctly in his comprehensive theological introduction to Scripture, *The Institutes of the Christian Religion,* and the development of the doctrine can be traced in the various editions of the book. In the earliest text of the *Institutes,* dated 1535 and published in Basel in 1536, Calvin challenges the traditional definition of the diaconate on the basis of his biblical studies. He speaks of the diaconate as an ecclesiastical ministry of charity and rejects the traditional liturgical interpretation.

> The origin, ordination, and office of the deacons are described by Luke in the Acts [Acts 6:3]. . . . This was the office of deacons: to attend to the care of the poor and minister to them; from this they took their name. For they are so called, as ministers. . . . Paul also speaks of the deacons: he wishes them to be modest, not double-tongued, not wine-bibbers, not pursuing filthy gain, well established in the faith [1 Tim. 3:8-9], husbands of one wife, governing their households and children well [1 Tim. 3:12]. But* what likeness to this is there in the deacons which these men devise? . . . They say that it is the office of their deacons to "assist the priests; to minister in everything done in the sacraments. . . ." Is there one word here of the true ministry of deacons?[5]

The enlarged edition of the *Institutes* published in 1539 adds little to this description, but the revisions and expansions in 1543 set out the whole teaching clearly. As was quoted in the discussion of plural ministries in chapter two above, Calvin states that the diaconate is a permanent office.[6] The following is a description of the office itself.

> The care of the poor was entrusted to the deacons. However, two kinds are mentioned in the letter to the Romans: "He that gives, let him do it with simplicity; . . . he that shows mercy, with cheerfulness" [Rom. 12:8]. Since it is certain that Paul is speaking of the public office of the church, there must have been two distinct grades. Unless my judgment deceive me, in the first clause he designates the deacons who distribute the alms. But the second refers to those who had devoted themselves to the care of the poor and sick. Of this sort were the widows whom Paul mentions to Timothy [1 Tim. 5:9-10]. Women could fill no other public office than to devote themselves to the care of the poor. If we accept this (as it must be accepted), there will be two kinds of deacons: one to serve the church in administering the affairs of the poor; the other, in caring for the poor themselves. But even though the term *diakonia* itself has a wider application, Scripture specifically designates as deacons those whom the church has appointed to distribute alms

and take care of the poor, and serve as stewards of the common chest of the poor. Their origin, institution, and office are described by Luke in The Acts [Acts 6:3]. For when the Greeks started a rumor that their widows were being neglected in the relief of the poor, the apostles, making the excuse that they were unable to fulfill both functions (preaching the Word and serving at table), asked the multitude to choose seven upright men to whom they might entrust this task [Acts 6:1ff]. Here, then, is the kind of deacons the apostolic church had, and which we, after their example, should have.[7]

Calvin believed that he drew his teaching from the Bible, and certainly his treatment of the diaconate in the *Institutes* appeals to Scripture as its foundation. A study of the way the Reformer explained the many biblical passages to which he refers can illuminate whence Calvin drew the specific features of the diaconate and how he consciously and conscientiously developed his theology.

DEVELOPMENT OF THE ADMINISTRATIVE DEACONS: ACTS 6:1-6 AND 1 TIMOTHY 3:8-13

The organization of Calvin's teaching on the diaconate, like its development, can be examined in two main stages, focused on the two kinds of diaconal personnel. The first and most important part of the Calvinist Reformed diaconate may be seen as an expanded study of the biblical references in the earliest edition of the *Institutes*. The first of the two key Scripture texts on which Calvin's diaconate is based is Acts 6:1-6:

> Now in these days, when the number of the disciples was multiplying, there arose a murmuring of the Grecian Jews against the Hebrews, because their widows were neglected in the daily ministration. And the twelve called the multitude of the disciples unto them, and said, It is not fit that we should forsake the word of God, and serve tables. Look ye out therefore, brethren, from among you seven men of good report, full of the Spirit and of wisdom, whom we may appoint over this business. But we will continue stedfastly in prayer, and in the ministry of the word. And the saying pleased

the whole multitude: and they chose Stephen, a man full of faith and of the Holy Spirit, and Philip, and Prochorus, and Nicanor, and Timon and Parmenas, and Nicolas a proselyte of Antioch: whom they set before the apostles: and when they had prayed, they laid their hands on them.[8]

The second text is 1 Timothy 3:8-13:

> Deacons in like manner must be grave, not double tongued, not given to much wine, not greedy of filthy lucre; holding the mystery of the faith in a pure conscience. And let these also first be proved; then let them serve as deacons, if they be blameless. Women in like manner must be grave, not slanderers, temperate, faithful in all things. Let deacons be husbands of one wife, ruling their children and their own houses well. For they that have served well as deacons gain to themselves a good standing, and great boldness in the faith which is in Christ Jesus.[9]

Calvin's choice of biblical texts followed all of Christian history. As is evident from reading the two passages quoted, the name "deacon" appears only in the second one. At least from the end of the first century, though, the seven chosen to serve tables were understood as deacons. But the way in which the church explained and applied the Scriptures which were identified as diaconal was not always precisely the same. A very brief sketch of the main features in the history of the interpretation of each text provides a context for understanding Calvin's use of these passages.

Although both Acts 6 and 1 Timothy 3 were important in traditional teaching on the diaconate, the latter text seems to have been given the greater weight in medieval times. Along with the greeting to the "bishops and deacons" in Philippians 1:1, the association of these two offices in 1 Timothy 3:1-13 clearly established them as similar ecclesiastical ministries. The virtues required of the deacon in verses 8-13 are similar to those of the bishop in verses 1-7. In addition, most discussions of the "good rank" ("good standing") in verse 13 interpreted this reward as promotion from the diaconate to the episcopate. In actual practice, deacons normally became priests, but the principle of promotion in holy orders is clear. As we might expect, the reference to deacons' wives in verse 11 caused some debate, though not for the reasons one might suppose. Apparently this was a key text used by the early Christian sect of Montanism to support the ordination or ministry of women. Most commentators who mention this idea flatly reject it, though they calmly acknowledge that in the early church and among Eastern Christians deacons might marry.

Although 1 Timothy 3 makes no explicit mention of the deacon's task, this was plainly understood as liturgical and "spiritual." Reconciling this conviction with the text of Acts 6, in which the seven are chosen for the "temporal" task of serving tables, presented a problem for medieval exegetes. Not only did the seven handle mundane business, but the apostles laid hands on them for this work. A number of explanations for this action were offered over the course of time. Laying on of hands was the rite for ordination, but one could only be ordained for a spiritual task. Therefore, some biblical scholars suggested that hands were laid on the deacons when spiritual duties were added to the temporal ones mentioned in Acts. Given their conviction that only the spiritual can be a proper ecclesiastical office, medieval theologians could not finally resolve the exegetical problem of Acts 6 and leaned more heavily on the Pauline epistles for their doctrine of the diaconate.

Protestants of the sixteenth century continued to understand both Acts 6 and 1 Timothy 3 as diaconal passages, but unlike the earlier tradition, they made Acts the dominant voice. Convinced by the doctrine of justification by faith alone that nothing which God created is profane in itself, Protestants had no difficulty in accepting the idea that the apostles had handled temporal business. Nor did they object to the laying on of hands for setting apart to a mundane task. Laying on of hands is a biblical rite for consecration but it does not effect anything, as Calvin explained clearly.

> The laying on of hands was a solemn symbol of consecration under the Law. The apostles now place their hands on the deacons for

this purpose, that they may know that they are being dedicated to God. Because the ceremony was empty in itself, however, there is added at the same time a prayer, in which the faithful commend to God the ministers whom they are presenting to Him. This is certainly ascribed to the apostles, for the whole of the people did not lay their hands on the deacons, but when the apostles said prayers on behalf of the Church the others added theirs. We gather from this that the laying on of hands is a rite consistent with order and dignity, seeing that it was used by the apostles; not of course that it has any efficacy or virtue in itself, but its power and effect depend solely on the Spirit of God.[10]

Some Protestants, for example, Zwinglians, eliminated laying on of hands entirely; others, for instance, Lutherans, used it for the pastoral ministry, the only ecclesiastical ministry they recognized. Although Genevan authorities refused to allow it to be practiced, Calvin considered laying on of hands appropriate for the ordination of pastors, teachers, and deacons, and he would have liked to reinstitute it.[11]

The primary point about Acts 6 for Protestants, however, was its definition of the task of the diaconate, and secondarily the effect of this definition on the interpretation of 1 Timothy 3. The seven were elected to care for the poor, not to assist a priest with the liturgy. In their discussions of 1 Timothy 3, almost all Protestants refer to Acts 6 to explain the work of the diaconate, which the epistle does not delineate. One consequence of this explanation of 1 Timothy by Acts was that many Protestants objected to explaining the "good rank" in 1 Timothy 3:13 as a promotion from deacon to presbyter. Experience in a diaconate of social concern did not fit one to be promoted to the ministry of the Word; both are important kinds of service but they require different gifts. Calvin's own comment on verse 13 insists that the "good rank" means praise for faithful ministry as a deacon.

> I for my part, without denying that the diaconate may sometimes be the nursery from which presbyters are chosen, yet prefer a simpler explanation of Paul's words, that those who have dis-

charged this ministry well are worthy of no small honour, for it is not a menial task but a highly honourable office. By so speaking he makes it clear how profitable it is for the Church to have this work done by carefully chosen men, for the holy performance of its duties procures esteem and reverence.[12]

Thus most Protestant biblical commentators interpreted Acts 6 and 1 Timothy 3 as describing the ministry of relief for the poor in the early church.

General agreement on interpretation, however, did not necessarily mean that all Protestants drew the same conclusions about the contemporary significance of the teaching in these biblical texts. Many of these commentators, especially Lutherans and Zwinglians, did not consider the church order of the New Testament necessarily prescriptive for all time. Care of the poor was clearly always very important, but it need not be ecclesiastical in the strict sense. The office of deacon known to the apostolic church could (Lutheran) or should (Zwinglian) be handled by the Christian ruler now that Christianity was legally established.

For the Calvinist Reformed tradition, though, the ecclesiastical ministry of charity in the early church was intended as the pattern for the church throughout time. A few quotations from Calvin's commentaries and sermons on Acts 6 and 1 Timothy 3 can highlight certain important aspects of the teaching summarized earlier in the chapter. The work of the deacon is definitely a ministry of benevolence.

> We now ascertain the purpose for which deacons were created. The term itself is certainly a general one, yet it is properly taken for the stewards of the poor.[13]

The ministry to the poor is clearly an ecclesiastical service.

> All who are elected to distribute alms and to govern the property of the poor, are not only in a public position but they belong to the spiritual government of the Church, and they are there as officers of God, in order to distribute the sacrifices which are offered and consecrated to Him.[14]

The diaconate is not primarily a liturgical office, but the early church practice of giving deacons some role in worship in token of their status as ministers is appropriate.

> We see how they are strictly commanded to walk as before God, to think about the fact that their office was not secular or worldly but in fact a spiritual task. For this reason it was given to the deacons to offer the cup when the people came to the Supper of our Lord Jesus Christ. Those who had the responsibility of the poor were there joined with the ministers of the Word of God, in order that they might be recognized as having a task in the Church, and they themselves might recognize that they must walk uprightly, as if to say: "We are no longer our own, but we must dedicate ourselves wholly to the service of God."[15]

The ministry to the poor is not only clearly ecclesiastical but it is also distinct from the presbyterial ministry. The deacon is the minister of the church, not the servant of the pastor.

> The different interpretations [of the diaconate] need not occasion us any doubt. It is certain that the apostle is referring to men who hold public office in the Church and this refutes the view of those who think that by deacons he means domestic servants [such as medieval bishops employed for financial matters].[16]

This ministry of the church to the poor and sick was intended to be permanent. Although not every story in Scripture is a model for Christian behavior,[17] when a narrative such as Luke's account of the seven corresponds to a general rule such as Paul's command to Timothy about deacons, the biblical history is intended as normative for the church.

> And in fact, if we observe how St. Paul speaks of it, we will find he makes it a general rule. He does not merely tell a story, as St. Luke does here, in order to show us by example what ought to be done, but he says to Timothy: "This is how you shall ordain deacons." . . . It is true that it is sometimes considered an office of small importance to serve God by serving the poor. But St. Paul says that it is an excellent rank, indeed a freedom in the faith to those who have walked rightly in this task. Therefore, we can apply St. Paul's passage to St. Luke's discussion, which thus not merely tells us a story about what was done once, but

shows us that this ought to be a lasting order in the Church of God: that those who are established to rule the Church should have the care of the poor. . . .

Let us return to ourselves and recognize why this history is told to us. God informs us what government, order, and organization He wants to command to be among His own. For if we want to be considered His church we must have what is here proclaimed to us. And what His apostles did must be a lasting example to us, since we have a general rule about it from the mouth of St. Paul. He not only shows us what the apostles did, but look! he says, what all Christians ought to do if they want Jesus Christ to reign and there to be order in the church: it is necessary that the poor be cared for, and for this there must be deacons.[18]

Thus, for Calvin and the Reformed tradition which followed him, the ecclesiastical ministry of care for the poor and sick is a necessary and permanent office of the Christian church.

DEVELOPMENT OF THE WOMEN DEACONS: ROMANS 16:1-2 AND 1 TIMOTHY 5:3-10

The development of the second part of Calvin's diaconate can perhaps best be understood as the solution to some problems of biblical interpretation. The Reformer took seriously the task of explaining all of Scripture, so he could not skip any texts. Since he believed that the New Testament church had a unified order which was the model for later times, all the awkward passages had to be fitted together and explained in relationship to the clear ones. In addition, traditional interpretations which were manifestly wrong must be corrected. The two principal biblical texts on which Calvin based his second sort of deacon were problem passages, for which the Reformer's solutions are fully in character with his methodology. (They are also remarkably imaginative, if not wholly convincing explanations.)

The first and probably more important problem Calvin faced was explaining the text of Romans 16:1-2, which calls a woman a "deacon."

> I commend unto you Phoebe our sister, who is a servant [*diakonos*] of the church that is at Cenchreae: that ye receive her in the Lord, worthily of the saints, and that ye assist her in whatsoever matter she may have need of you: for she herself also hath been a succourer of many, and of mine own self.[19]

It was plain from other Scriptures (Acts 6 and 1 Timothy 3) that the diaconate was a permanent ecclesiastical office with certain duties, so the fact that Phoebe was called a "deacon" could not be explained away even if Calvin had been willing to skip inconvenient passages. Phoebe's work was also clearly a form of *diakonia*, though a service slightly different from that ascribed to the seven in Acts. Calvin's comment on Phoebe is straightforward in recognizing her public ministry.

> [Paul] begins by commending Phoebe, the bearer of the epistle, first on account of her office, because she exercised a very honourable and holy ministry in the Church. The second reason, he suggests, which should make it their duty to welcome her and show her every kindness, is that she has always devoted herself to all the godly. . . . It is fitting that we should not only embrace with affection all members of Christ, but also respect and bestow particular love and honour upon those who exercise any public office in the Church.[20]

An explanation of Phoebe's diaconal status had to be found, however, and for one accustomed as Calvin was to interpreting Scripture by Scripture, there were clues. As other commentators had noted, Phoebe's service (often interpreted as hospitality) resembles rather closely that of the widows discussed in 1 Timothy 5:3, 5, 9-10.

> Honour widows that are widows indeed. . . . Now she that is a widow indeed and desolate hath her hope set on God, and continueth in supplications and prayers night and day. . . . Let none be enrolled as a widow under threescore years old, having been the wife of one man, well reported for good works; if she hath brought up children, if she hath used hospitality to strangers, if she hath washed the saints' feet, if she hath relieved the afflicted, if she hath diligently followed every good work.[21]

In fact, the Timothy passage on widows was another problem text for Calvin. Traditionally the women in 1 Timothy 5 had been considered nuns, and these verses were used as a text to prove vows of celibacy. Calvin, like other Protestants, strongly objected to this Roman Catholic interpretation, but he could not simply deny it. He had to provide his own positive explanation, not only to counter the Roman one but also because, according to his own principles, 1 Timothy 5, like chapter 3, was a general rule.

Calvin solved the problems of both Romans 16 and 1 Timothy 5 by linking Phoebe and the widows together as a kind of diaconal order charged with a personal ministry to the tangible needs of the saints.

> The character of the ministry which he is discussing [in Rom. 16:1] is also described in 1 Tim. 5:10. The poor were supported out of the public funds of the Church, and were looked after by persons charged with that duty. For this last widows were chosen who, since they were free from domestic duties and not hindered by children, desired to dedicate themselves wholly to God for religious service. They were therefore received into this office to which they were bound and under obligation, just as one who hires his services ceases to be free and to be his own master.[22]

So Calvin understood Phoebe and the widows as the female deacons of the New Testament, charged with the personal care of the sick and the poor. Nonetheless, one problem remained to be explained. How were these women related to the administrators of Acts 6 and 1 Timothy 3?

THE COORDINATION OF THE TWOFOLD DIACONATE: ROMANS 12:8

The most controversial text on which Calvin based his twofold diaconate is Romans 12:8, one of the three lists of ministerial functions discussed in the earlier chapter on a plurality of ministries. The Reformer explained this verse for the first time in his commentary on Romans, completed in 1539 and published in the next year.

> When Paul speaks here of givers *(metadidoúntas)*, he does not mean those who give their own possessions, but technically the deacons who are charged with the distribution of the public property of the Church. When he speaks of those who show mercy *(eleoúntas)*, he means widows and other ministers, who were appointed to take care of the sick, according to the custom of the ancient church. There are two diverse functions, to provide what is necessary for the poor and to look after them. On the former he impresses *simplicity*, by which they are to administer faithfully what was entrusted to them without fraud or respect of persons. From the latter he desires a display of compliance with *cheerfulness*, that they may not, as very often happens, spoil the services which they render by their morose attitude.[23]

A number of explanations have been offered for Calvin's rather peculiar interpretation of Romans 12:8.[24] Some scholars think that the Genevan Reformer was simply using the best biblical warrant he could find to explain, enhance, and perhaps influence the civil welfare system. The fact that his twofold diaconate developed after Calvin became acquainted with the Genevan system certainly makes such an idea logical and persuasive. Several other scholars have suggested either that Calvin's two kinds of deacons (as well as the plural ministry idea) were adopted from Martin Bucer, or that Bucer and Calvin developed the four-office system (with its double diaconate) as an almost accidental consequence of the theory of plural ministries. These last two explanations do not take into account the different ways that Bucer and Calvin treat the second kind of deacon, nor the fact that other biblical texts compelled the Reformers to teach at least a single kind of diaconate. Also, none of these explanations appears to give adequate attention to the history of interpretation of Romans 12:8 and the complex of scriptural texts associated with this verse in Calvin's comprehensive discussion of the diaconate in the *Institutes*.

Calvin's explanation of Romans 12:8 can be understood

as a development of a stream of interpretation inherited from his predecessors, which was in fact passed on to later commentators in a variety of religious communities. The first notable forerunner of the Genevan Reformer's peculiar explanation of Romans 12:8 was the Christian humanist (and Roman Catholic reformer) Jacques Lefèvre d'Étaples. Perhaps drawing on a hint in the medieval writer William of St. Thierry, Lefèvre's commentary of 1512 explained Romans 12:6-8 as a series of gifts appropriate to special civil and ecclesiastical offices. His notes on "those who give aid" and "those who do mercy" sound very much like the later Reformed comments on these diaconal phrases.

Among the Protestant commentaries on Romans are several early Reformed ones which Calvin certainly read. In 1525, the Basel theologian John Oecolampadius published a commentary on Romans, in which he treated Romans 12:6-8 as a series of different ecclesiastical functions or offices. In commenting on verse 8, Oecolampadius also changed the order of the phrases to juxtapose the two diaconal ones as clearly related tasks. The interpretation of Romans 12:6-8 was carried further by Calvin's friend Martin Bucer. The Strasbourg Reformer explicitly affirmed that in this passage Paul was naming public offices of the church. Bucer also significantly reduced the number of offices to five: three presbyterial functions and two diaconal ones. Bucer did not connect Phoebe and the widows with this explanation of Romans 12:8, nor did he develop further or use systematically the idea of a double diaconate. Calvin, however, did.

Calvin adopted and applied consistently Bucer's interpretation of Romans 12:8, apparently because it enabled him to explain the relationship of Phoebe and the widows to the deacons of Acts 6 and 1 Timothy 3. "Those who give aid," that is, handle the finances of the poor, are the seven (male) administrators who were chosen to manage the ministry to the needy. "Those who do mercy" are the (female) nurses who exercised hospitality and served the poor personally. The idea that Romans 12:8 was used to explain the relationship of two kinds of deacons also fits with the development of the biblical texts cited in various editions of the *Institutes'* discussion of the diaconate. The reference to 1 Timothy 3, which is found in the earliest editions of the *Institutes,* is *replaced* by a reference to 1 Timothy 5 in 1543. At the same time that this reference to the widows appears, the Romans 12:8 text is also added.

A few questions remain. Why were there no widow deacons in Geneva? Calvin's sermons on 1 Timothy 5:3ff., preached to the Genevan people in 1555, indicate his real regret that their church had no widow deacons. He was, however, chiefly concerned that the poor be cared for, that the functions of the second kind of deacon be carried out, and the hospitaller of the city system and the deacons of the refugee organizations fulfilled these duties adequately. Diaconal *functions* were more important than the precise personnel who carried out this service to the needy.

The second question, why Calvin subordinated the women deacons to the men, is considered below in the context of the Reformer's discussion of women in church leadership.

CRITIQUE OF CALVIN'S TEACHING ON THE DIACONATE

The strengths and weaknesses of John Calvin's teaching on the diaconate can be assessed from various viewpoints. The Reformer's greatest strength in this as in all his work was unquestionably his determination to be faithful to the sole authority of Scripture and to all of Scripture, his refusal to skip inconvenient passages.

Calvin's most significant weakness, his sometimes contorted explanation of biblical texts, is a direct corollary of his strength. Some of the reasons for the Reformer's occasionally farfetched interpretations of Scripture cannot be blamed on the man himself. Although he was in fact considerably more perceptive than most of his contemporaries, the Genevan Reformer was a man of his own times. He had no reason to question the conviction (shared by almost all people at least to the eighteenth century) that Scripture is a unified whole, and that the New Testament in particular describes a single, fully organized ecclesiastical community.

Calvin also was not unusual in regarding the earliest church as the model for subsequent ages. He was not a literalist, set upon restoring every detail of the apostolic time. Indeed, Calvin had a high regard for the fact that the church on earth lives in history and therefore is necessarily concrete, "embodied," but he was convinced that there are right (biblical) and wrong ways to embody revelation. The tangible external aids to salvation, especially the church's worship and ministry, are too important to have been left to human judgment. Calvin insisted repeatedly that the Holy Spirit has shown how God wishes to be worshiped and served, and it is idolatry to set up our own ways instead. Through Scripture God has given general rules for the organization of Christian worship and church order, and the task of the church's faithful teachers is to gather and explain these instructions. Calvin's fault was a determination to be more consistent and thorough than most other theologians in fitting together the discrete passages. Sometimes this determination meant a creative or imaginative approach to the puzzle of fitting one text with another, as he struggled to establish what he believed was the biblical and right pattern of church order, including the office of deacon.

Absolute uniformity is not necessary for ecumenical fellowship. Calvin clearly recognized as Christian brothers and sisters people who disagreed with him on church order and liturgical forms, and he was willing to compromise on some things for the sake of Christian fellowship.[25] He continued, though, to believe that there are better and worse, more and less faithful, ways to act on revelation, and he strove for what he saw as better and more faithful.

If we can understand Calvin's convictions regarding the unity of the New Testament church order and its normative status, another critical difficulty in his doctrine of the diaconate is the question of women's participation. This second major problem can best be treated as a part of the wider discussion of women in ecclesiastical leadership.

CALVIN ON WOMEN IN CHURCH LEADERSHIP, ESPECIALLY WOMEN IN THE DIACONATE

The usual image of Calvin is that of a rigid, patriarchal tyrant who saw society and especially women as part of a divinely ordered hierarchy from which only rebels and sinners seek to escape. In fact, although he was certainly socially conservative in practice, the Genevan Reformer's theory had considerably more flexibility than popular lore—and the codification of his theory by less gifted successors—have led us to believe.

The excellent book, *Women, Freedom, and Calvin,* by Jane Dempsey Douglass, sets the discussion of Calvin's teaching on women in the appropriate theological context, the doctrine of Christian freedom.[26] As was seen earlier, one of the key insights of the Protestant Reformation was the "freedom of a Christian," the title of Martin Luther's manifesto. Placing Calvin's teaching on women in this context, therefore, reminds us properly that this question is a corollary of what lies at the heart of the Protestant revisioning of Christian theology. Before we narrow the focus to the effect on the status of women, it is helpful to sketch Calvin's teaching on Christian freedom.

The Christian is free in three ways. First, we are freed from the condemnation of the law because we are justified by faith alone. Christ's righteousness has been reckoned to our account and we are accepted as if we were righteous. This is sheer grace, given to us through faith. The second sort of freedom is the freedom of the third use of the law, the freedom to follow the law as far as possible, in service to the neighbor. This is never a perfect fulfillment of the law, of course, and it earns nothing. It allows our gratitude for grace to find expression. *Diakonia* is perhaps the clearest manifestation of this second kind of Christian freedom.

The third part of Christian freedom, proposed by Philipp Melanchthon, became very important in the Reformed tradition.

According to this teaching, many things and activities do not fall into the category either of command or of prohibition. We might say that these things are morally neutral; the Reformation term was "indifferent things," *adiaphora*, things which are good or bad depending upon how we use them. In sixteenth-century Protestantism, one common indifferent thing was fasting. Fasting is obviously a biblical practice, but Protestants thought that it had been very much abused by the medieval church, and thus it was no longer really indifferent. Fasting was rejected as a means of earning merit. Rightly understood as a means of self-discipline and not as a good work, however, fasting was still approved and practiced by Protestants.

To the surprise of many modern readers, Douglass has pointed out (or reminded us) that Calvin considered women's silence in church (1 Cor. 14:34) an "indifferent thing." Calvin saw women's subordination as right according to the order of nature, and he regarded a context in which women spoke publicly as disorderly. However, Calvin did acknowledge that the Holy Spirit is a higher authority than the order of nature, and ideas of order and decorum might change. Thus, Calvin alone among mainline Protestants put the question of women's leadership in the church in the category of indifferent things, from the first edition of the *Institutes* to the last. The section from 1536 is worth quoting.

> Nor can Paul's requirement—that "all things be done decently and in order"—be met unless order itself and decorum be established through the addition of observances that form, as it were, a bond of union. But . . . these observances . . . are not to be considered necessary for salvation. . . . [They] pertain only to the decorum with which all things should be done in the assembly of believers in fitting order, or to keep that community of men within bounds by some sort of bonds of humanity. . . .
>
> There are examples of the first sort [of decorous ordinance] in Paul: that women should not teach in the church [1 Cor. 14:34], that they should go out with heads covered [1 Cor. 11:5ff.]. And examples can be seen in the everyday habits of living, such as: that we pray with knees bent and head bare.[27]

If Calvin could regard women's leadership in the church as not opposed in theory to God's will, and if he recognized that Scripture gives a place to women in the diaconate, why was his practice so conservative? The chief answer is that Calvin was a man of his own age; he shared the assumptions of his day about the canons of decency and order. It was simply not decorous or edifying to have women lead in the church, though Calvin never criticized the early Protestant women in Geneva who in fact preached during the days of upheaval at the beginning of the city's reformation. Thus Calvin the sixteenth-century man could state that the only decorous public role possible for women was as nurses for the sick and poor.

A second reason for Calvin's subordinating the female deacons (Phoebe and the widows) to the male administrators may have been influenced by the New Testament passages themselves. The seven in Acts 6 are clearly ordained by laying on of hands, something not given to the widows in 1 Timothy. It is likely that Calvin also saw the widows' service of hospitality as a more private and less independent task than that of the deacons who determined how money should be spent. The cultural factor was more critical than the biblical interpretation, however. The weight of the cultural conservatism is evident in the fact that, apparently because he was a man, the male Genevan hospitaller (the second sort of deacon) shared with the procurators (the administrators) the diaconal privilege of offering the cup at the Lord's Supper.[28]

On the other side of the question, it may be said that Calvin was probably the only Protestant who gave women a place in the regular ministry of the church. Other reformers, especially Anabaptists, allowed inspired women to speak, but Calvin appears to be the only one to give women a role in the *offices* of ministry not based on charismatic gifts. It was certainly a subordinate role in the regular ministry, an unordained office, but it was a place in the structure.

In conclusion, it may be said that Calvin's theory was less culturally conditioned than his practice. One cannot say what Calvin would do if he lived in the twentieth century, but it is

81

possible to point out the ways his thought could be developed in accordance with its own inherent tendencies. Driven by the biblical texts of Romans and 1 Timothy, Calvin included women in his regular ministerial offices, though for cultural and biblical reasons he made these deacons subordinate to the male deacons. Explaining Paul's injunction to women to remain silent in the church as an indifferent thing, a question of order which might change with new ideas of edification and decency, Calvin at least theoretically opened the door to a reconsideration of women's leadership in every aspect of church life if a time came when ideas of decorum were different. The present is such a time, and if Calvinist theory and practice are made consistent, women can and should be welcomed not only as full deacons equal with men, but also as equal in all aspects of church leadership.

Chapter Five

DEACONS AND *DIAKONIA* SINCE THE REFORMATION

With the discovery of the priesthood of all believers in the reformation of the sixteenth century new vistas for understanding the Christian life opened up. In the gradual discovery of the diaconate of all believers the reformation continued. While the seventeenth century was still very much concerned with consolidating the reform of the Church in systems of orthodoxy, the eighteenth century began to interpret the reformation in new experiments of Christian living. Since then diakonia as a core concept of the Christian faith slowly moved across the consciousness-threshold of the Church.

F. Herzog, "Diakonia in Modern Times"[1]

DIAKONIA IS ESSENTIAL to the life of the church, and it may exist with or without a formal diaconal office in church order. According to the classical Reformed tradition, however, an ecclesiastical diaconate is one necessary expression of the diaconal responsibility of the church as a worshiping body, an institution. Over the centuries since the Protestant Reformation, along with the spread of new diaconal movements, the Reformed tradition has attempted to keep some kind of tie between Christian *diakonia* and an office of diaconal leadership. At some times the effort has been successful. At other times a moribund or confused diaconate has been called to account by the vigor of nonecclesiastical *diakonia*. Christians in the late twentieth century celebrate the joy of expanding ecumenical service in the world and also envision a coming together again of *diakonia* and the church's diaconate.

The present chapter offers a brief sketch of a few major developments in diaconal thought and activity between Calvin's day and ours. The story is painted with large brush strokes, and it gives most attention to the Anglo-American branches of the Reformed tradition. The focus is first the diaconate as an institution or office, then the various expressions of *diakonia* which extend beyond any formal ecclesiastical structure. Other traditions besides the Reformed are mentioned; however, there is no attempt to be exhaustive. The discussion concludes with a somewhat more detailed examination of the late twentieth-century *Baptism, Eucharist and Ministry* document and some of the ongoing responses to this ecumenical statement. The whole chapter should be understood as an impressionistic painting intended to explain for Reformed (especially American) Christians something of what happened to the Calvinist diaconate between the time of its classical formulation in the sixteenth century and the quest for the diaconate in the contemporary ecumenical church.

THE REFORMED DIACONATE IN THE SIXTEENTH AND SEVENTEENTH CENTURIES

For many years the connection between the diaconate as office and *diakonia* as service remained strong in the Reformed church, although *diakonia* was not confined to church structures.

One good place to find what Reformed Christians believed about *diakonia* in the church is in confessional statements on the diaconate. Examination of various theological writings and church orders makes it clear that the Calvinist definition of the diaconate, and even the characteristic biblical texts, continued to mold Reformed thought. Examples from the English Puritan and Scottish Presbyterian branches of the tradition are particularly interesting to a North American audience, although Dutch Calvinist and French Huguenot sources are also closely linked with this part of the Reformed family.

One after another, the confessions repeat the fourfold Calvinist organization of plural ministries, often with the double diaconate included.[2] Practice also at first followed theory. Indeed, some few churches, such as those in the Rhineland, even instituted female deacons or widows. The best-known instance of a woman deacon in the English world is found in an account by Governor Bradford of the pilgrim congregation in London and Amsterdam.

> She honored her place . . . and was an ornament to the congregation. She usually sat in a convenient place in the congregation, with a little birchen rod in her hand, and kept little children in great awe from disturbing the congregation. She did frequently visit the sick and weak, especially women, and as there was need, called out maids and young women to watch and do them other helps as their necessity did require; and if they were poor, she would gather relief for them of those that were able, or acquaint the deacons; and she was obeyed as a mother in Israel and an officer of Christ.[3]

Early in the seventeenth century, however, women deacons were dropped from the few churches which had them, and references to them also began to disappear from the confessions. The diaconate as such, though, continued to be strongly affirmed, and the Reformed practice even spread to some other communities, for example, from Dutch Reformed to Dutch, English, and (later) American Lutherans.[4]

Alongside the formal diaconates of the churches, Reformed Christians were also concerned with *diakonia* in a more generalized sense. As studies of England illustrate, the impulse toward benevolence was apparently given vigorous encouragement by Protestantism. Acting on the conviction that the holy may be found anywhere, and one's calling is the place to serve

God, Protestants continued the Calvinist penchant for saturating daily life with moral considerations.[5] The so-called Protestant work ethic is well known. What is less often remembered is that the fruits of this work were not normally hoarded, much less consumed extravagantly. Indeed, the fruits were often devoted to public causes, to various forms of service to the community. Often the attitude was distinctly paternalistic, but the social improvement was frequently quite real.[6]

THE EIGHTEENTH AND NINETEENTH CENTURIES

Formal diaconates continued in many Reformed churches, but over time in some places their sense of purpose and effectiveness decreased, and other forms of *diakonia* developed. This change occurred especially in the new world, with its very different ecclesiastical and civil conditions, and the following discussion focuses particularly on North America.

The confusion about the diaconate in North America is one place to begin a sketch of the changing situation. By the early eighteenth century, Cotton Mather in New England saw the diaconate as redundant and practically speaking unnecessary. Many early Presbyterian churches in North America were organized without diaconates, although problems with the offices of deacon and elder were a matter of concern to some people.[7] Contributing to the difficulties with the diaconate was a growing confusion about the precise nature and function of this office. Not a few Reformed groups in North America, especially those of Puritan background, retained either the Reformed elders' office or the deacons' office, but not both. Even more than in the earlier French Reformed tradition, the distinction between the two offices was blurred. Particularly those with a congregationalist polity tended to reject the office of elder but allocate to deacons some of the duties Calvin had assigned to elders. Sometimes the church's concern for the poor and needy thus became muted or overwhelmed in a host of other important duties of communal care.[8]

One frequent result of the general ambiguity about the

duties of the diaconate was the development of church trustees to handle finances. Whether or not some theological basis was found for these boards of trustees (my limited reading has turned up only pragmatic justifications), the introduction of these church servants further complicated the situation. Trustees usually managed financial matters, especially support for the pastors and church upkeep, which had once been part of the deacons' task. (Early disestablished Reformed churches commonly had separate collections for church support and relief of the poor, but both were normally managed by deacons.) To complicate matters further, some trustees eventually carried out duties originally associated with the Reformed elder.[9]

Confusion about the diaconate increased in the eighteenth and nineteenth centuries, even while active *diakonia* on many levels was flourishing more widely. The growth of often non-ecclesiastical diaconal action is an exciting story, and when this story is understood, the confusion in defining the office of deacon can be better comprehended.

The great religious discovery of the eighteenth century, developed in full glory by the nineteenth, was the awakening or revival.[10] The waves of spiritual renewal swept across Western European and North American Protestantism, winning souls and organizing new churches. Especially in the nineteenth century, converts were urged to put their faith to work in practical fashion, to act in ways that would express and spread their convictions. Rather naturally, then, *diakonia* flourished in areas where the awakening was strong. The nineteenth century in North America is an amazing scene to contemplate.

Revival measures and perfectionist aspiration flourished increasingly between 1840 and 1865 in all the major denominations — particularly in the cities. And they drew together a constellation of ideas and customs which ever since have lighted the diverging paths of American Protestantism. Lay leadership, the drive toward interdenominational fellowship, the primacy of ethics over dogma, and the democritization of Calvinism were more nearly fruits of fervor than of reflection. The quest of personal holiness became in some ways a kind of plain man's transcen-

dentalism, which geared ancient creeds to the drive shaft of social reform. Far from disdaining earthly affairs, the evangelists
played a key role in the widespread attack upon slavery, poverty,
and greed. They thus helped prepare the way both in theory
and in practice for what later became known as the social
gospel.[11]

Voluntary societies were organized to carry out a wide
variety of religious activities. There were associations for everything: from Bible, tract, education, and missionary societies, to
reforms directed to the plight of the deaf, the blind, and the in-
sane, to crusades for the abolition of slavery and the struggle
for women's rights. Indeed, voluntary societies to attack every
perceived injustice, every known ill, flourished in nineteenth-
century North America with amazing luxuriance. The force of
religious renewal inspired and fed the social conscience of all
the lands touched by revival fervor.

Revivals were clearly immensely important for *diakonia,*
but the social and political climate in which revivals developed
contributed to confusion on the nature of the church and therefore of the church's diaconate. All across the Western world, individualism was encouraged by the Enlightenment. Separation
of church and state brought many advantages, both theological
and practical, but it also had some less helpful consequences.
In places, such as the new United States, where the civil government was ecclesiastically neutral, the voluntary character of
church membership was strikingly emphasized. With the success of individualistic revival techniques, the establishment of
separation of church and state, and increasing religious pluralism, especially though not exclusively in North America, the
understanding of the nature of the church was altered in a number of ways. Without conscious reflection, many people who
became Christian by conversion in the eighteenth- and nineteenth-century revivals adopted a view of the church as a voluntary organization like other voluntary organizations, with significant consequences for *diakonia.*

In what sense is the church a voluntary association and
why should this affect its understanding of *diakonia?* The church

is a voluntary organization in two ways. In a secular society the church is voluntary in the sense that no civil power is exerted to force a person to be a member of a religious body. This legal distinction between citizenship and religious affiliation might be called "civil voluntarism," and nineteenth-century Reformed Christians like Alexandre Vinet of Switzerland led in the *religious* justification of separation of church and state.[12] The second kind of voluntarism is a different matter, however; indeed, it is a problem for the doctrine of the church. Along with and under cover of civil voluntarism, there came what might be called "theological voluntarism." Crudely expressed, "theological voluntarism" assumes that the church is established by like-minded people covenanting together to be a church. Carried to its logical conclusion, this definition of the church would imply that each covenanting group may define what it means to be the church— including whether *diakonia* is necessary—as if the nature of the church were not greater than individual decisions.

One of the several results of this unconscious theological voluntarism was that the strong impulse which the revivals gave to social concerns, as well as to evangelism, was not usually officially or structurally related to the churches (although the churches soon reclaimed the missionary societies). The separate, interdenominational nature of the reform societies need not have caused difficulties for *diakonia,* but sometimes it could. Social concerns were certainly not repudiated by church leadership—indeed, just the opposite—but they naturally developed separately from church structures. Usually churches encouraged their members to be morally conscientious, but Christians participated in the reform movement as individuals, and the precise connection between church membership and *diakonia* was rarely given adequate theological expression.

Another way to state this point is to say that churches did not oblige their members to take an interest in any particular social concerns; being a church member did not require one to be involved in corporate *diakonia.* Personal charity and kindness were naturally accepted as necessary, but the corporate obligation of *diakonia* did not receive clear theological recognition.

Many people, because they were Christians, were passionately concerned for their neighbors. However, because there was often no institutional ecclesiastical basis for the many diaconal activities of members, those who wanted to be only Sunday Christians were not called to account, not challenged to examine their own corporate diaconal responsibilities. The other side of this coin was the sense of some very committed Christian reformers that the church really was not obviously relevant to social change and the attack on injustice. Increasingly, as the nineteenth century passed and revival fervor waned, Christian reformers found their closest colleagues among secular humanists rather than among their fellow church members. The social gospel of the late nineteenth and early twentieth centuries illustrates clearly the struggle of Christians to be faithful and the difficulties of persuading the whole church to understand *diakonia* in corporate terms.[13] Not only the church's office of the diaconate, but also the relationship of Christian confession to Christian *diakonia,* was suffering from serious theological confusion by the early twentieth century.

Although the North American scene is in some ways the model for much of the way *diakonia* functions in the modern world of separation of church and state, the diaconal patterns of Protestant Western Europe in the nineteenth century are also important. In various established churches of Europe, two possibilities for diaconal renewal found expression. One was a voluntary pattern, somewhat similar to that in North America, except that being a voluntary association where churches are established is somewhat different from being one where the churches themselves are (in civil terms) voluntary societies. Where the established ecclesiastical leadership did not accept one revival-inspired project or another, voluntary societies were organized apart from the state churches.[14]

The second form of diaconal work in state or established churches was approved by the ecclesiastical authorities but rarely involved many people. Sometimes this *diakonia* was the renewal of an established Reformed diaconate, inspired by the revival movement. The best example of this diaconal work is found in nineteenth-century Scotland, where Thomas Chalmers briefly reinvigorated the church's diaconate to serve the new industrial poor. The work of Chalmers was strikingly effective for a short time, but managing national relief for the poor without state welfare did not succeed for long.[15]

Especially in Germany, but also in England and elsewhere, Christians outside the Reformed family, who had no tradition of an ecclesiastical diaconate of social concern, also sometimes founded new diaconal organizations. The names of the Lutherans Johann H. Wichern and Theodor Fliedner are particularly well known, though it is also important to remember the influence on these men of such reformers as the English Quaker Elizabeth Fry. Orders of deaconesses were thus organized as representatives of their churches. American branches of Lutheran and Methodist deaconess orders have continued devoted service for over a century.[16]

Nevertheless, relatively few Christians were personally involved in these formal orders of deaconesses. One of the key modern criticisms of this diaconal renewal movement is the fact that it allowed (if not encouraged) ordinary Christians to relegate the church's *diakonia* to specialists and to go their way without further personal concern.[17]

The diaconal heritage of the nineteenth century, both its strengths and its weaknesses, set the stage for the work of the twentieth century. A brief summary of the scene is therefore a useful prelude to the discussion of the more recent past.

The nineteenth century witnessed the expansion of diaconal concern among ordinary Christians. The widespread efforts to bring relief to all kinds of human ills resembles in some ways the virtually universal impulse toward individual charity found in the Middle Ages. Again, benevolent societies, like medieval confraternities, were from an ecclesiastical viewpoint voluntary associations. They were usually Christian, but not recognized as necessary expressions of the church's corporate life. Nevertheless, many of these reform societies clearly embodied a more concrete understanding of Christian service than some (many?) people found in their own churches.

Some churches also had various kinds of structures—somewhat like medieval religious orders—to carry out *diakonia*. As often happens in a large organization, individual members of these churches tended to relegate responsibility for charity or justice to these designated organs.

It is clear that concern for service to the neighbor flourished in nineteenth-century Christianity; it is also evident that not all was perfectly ordered. Many Christians practiced their *diakonia* completely separately from their church membership, or left ecclesiastical charity to special organs which could represent in a vicarious—and often remote—way their Christian duty of benevolence. In at least some measure, this fragmentation was a result of a kind of amnesia about the doctrine of the Church.

THE TWENTIETH CENTURY AND THE ECUMENICAL MOVEMENT

The most significant and exciting fact in twentieth-century Christianity is the rich and varied experience and expansion of the awakening from this amnesia, which is usually called "the ecumenical movement."[18] This renewed sense of the church, of its fundamental unity in Christ, has had an enormous impact on every aspect of Christian life and thought, not least on *diakonia*.

Theologically, the simplest way to express the significance of the ecumenical movement is as a renewal of ecclesiology, of the doctrine of the church as the one Body of Christ. One concrete manifestation of this reformation is a restored understanding of the church as God's creation, a body into which individuals are "engrafted," to use Calvin's term. The church is not created by our deciding to covenant together. The church has an identity and character given by Christ; it is Christ's Body and cannot be shaped according to our wishes any more than we could choose suddenly to have three legs and one arm, or two noses and no mouth. This givenness does not mean the church is a rigid entity; it is a body, living and growing. That the church is God's creation means that it is the nature of the church to be both gift and challenge to us. It is a gift because God has offered us the privilege of being members of Christ, members of God's family. It is a challenge because God's gift of the church does not allow us, its members, to pick and choose what arms or legs or other body parts we want or reject; it all comes together.[19]

The implications of the ecumenical movement for *diakonia* are many; only a few of the most important can be summarized here. Perhaps most vital is the fact that, if (as all believe) the nature of the church is to be a servant as Christ was a servant, then no Christian, no church member, can escape the obligation to *diakonia* and still claim to be faithful to Christ and the church. This point may not sound revolutionary in theory, but it can be rather discomforting or disturbing in practice. There will always be questions about what constitute necessary and appropriate expressions of *diakonia*. If we agree that *diakonia* makes claims on us because we are Christians, however, then we must face the fact that, once a thing is acknowledged as a proper expression of *diakonia,* we can ignore it only at the cost of denying in practice what we affirm in words. And this fact *is* revolutionary. A renewed sense of the essential, inescapable character of corporate *diakonia* is one of the most important contributions the ecumenical age has made, but the benefit has not all been one-way; the impulse to love the neighbor has also fostered unity.

Perhaps the most obvious relationship between ecumenism and *diakonia* has been the visible and practical acts of cooperation in service carried out together by different Christian communions. Perhaps the clearest evidence of this fact is the "Life and Work" movement, with its motto of "service unites," which contributed to the founding of the World Council of Churches. Shared service to the neighbor has provided pioneering leadership and encouragement in bringing Christians closer together in heart and mind. For many years one of the remarkable things about modern *diakonia* has been the fact that Christians who—tragically—could not pray together, could nevertheless serve together.

The practical *diakonia* of the modern world, like that of earlier times, has frequently worked through nonecclesiastical organizations. Often these parachurch diaconal agencies are developments from, or are modeled on, the nineteenth-century voluntary societies which sought to transform the world for Christ. Some of these contemporary "corporate deacons" are now related to ecclesiastical bodies or groups of denominations, sometimes through the World Council of Churches or national or regional councils, though many even of the religious ones are also (properly) still independent of any particular church connection. These practical, cooperative diaconal activities and organizations have contributed greatly to ecumenical understanding as well as to Christian witness, though sometimes the multitude of voluntary associations and the complexity of the relationship to church bodies has also created some confusion and competition, or at least duplication of efforts. Often voluntary societies, inspired by a new vision of what it means that Christ was a poor servant, have served as pioneers to challenge the more conservative ecclesiastical bodies, stirring up the imaginations of church members to see new fields of *diakonia*. In this connection it is appropriate to include some of the secular diaconal organizations, for example, the programs of civil governments or the agencies of the United Nations such as UNICEF, which Christians sometimes forget in their enumeration of service to the neighbor.[20]

BAPTISM, EUCHARIST AND MINISTRY AND THE QUEST FOR A TWENTIETH-CENTURY DIACONATE

Renewal of the teaching on the church as a servant and the experience of cooperative service in the world have led not only to a new age of *diakonia* but also to a new vision of the diaconate. Or perhaps it would be more accurate to say that there is a new quest for the diaconate, because clarity on the matter is still a considerable distance away. Along with other factors, such as the conviction that Christian disunity is an intolerable scandal, success in working together has led an increasingly wide variety of Christian confessions to discuss seriously what agreement on faith and order is possible. Clearly, the church's formal diaconate is a part of the order under discussion.

The most remarkable fruit of the ongoing quest for a common Christian proclamation is the document *Baptism, Eucharist and Ministry,* published in 1982 by the Faith and Order Commission of the World Council of Churches. (Although not a member of the World Council, the Roman Catholic Church is a full member of the Faith and Order Commission, so this document comes from a group of Roman Catholic, Orthodox, and Protestant theologians of many communions who have met and talked over a number of years.) After the publication of *Baptism, Eucharist and Ministry,* the so-called BEM document, member churches were requested to make official responses. The responses are being published exactly as they were submitted. I have examined a sampling of these comments, those found in the first three volumes containing answers from eighty-five churches. Certainly not all of the responses in this sample have remarked on the part of the document concerning the diaconate. Many have drawn attention to some aspect of this issue, however, and the various comments fall into several categories which suggest the state of the question today.

Baptism, Eucharist and Ministry itself discusses the diaconate briefly in the third and longest section, entitled "Ministry." First, the writers of BEM place the diaconate in the context of the calling of the whole people of God, the explanation of how an ordained ministry is related to the priesthood of believers, and the historical development of a threefold ordained ministry of bishops, priests, and deacons.[21] The need for a reform of the threefold pattern of ministry is plainly recognized, and is especially clear in the light of what has happened to the diaconate.

> In [other churches], the function of deacons has been reduced to an assistant role in the celebration of the liturgy: they have

ceased to fulfill any function with regard to the diaconal witness of the Church.[22]

Later in the document, the function of deacons is defined positively.

> *Deacons* represent to the Church its calling as servant in the world. By struggling in Christ's name with the myriad needs of societies and persons, deacons exemplify the interdependence of worship and service in the Church's life. They exercise responsibility in the worship of the congregation: for example by reading the scriptures, preaching and leading the people in prayer. They help in the teaching of the congregation. They exercise a ministry of love within the community. They fulfil certain administrative tasks and may be elected to responsibilities for governance.[23]

Along with the text of BEM there is printed a kind of unofficial commentary, which helps to explain the debates behind the text as formulated.

> In many churches there is today considerable uncertainty about the need, the rationale, the status and the functions of deacons. In what sense can the diaconate be considered part of the ordained ministry? What is it that distinguishes it from other ministries in the Church (catechists, musicians, etc.)? Why should deacons be ordained while these other ministries do not receive ordination? If they are ordained, do they receive ordination in the full sense of the word or is their ordination only the first step towards ordination as presbyters? Today, there is a strong tendency in many churches to restore the diaconate as an ordained ministry with its own dignity and meant to be exercised for life. As the churches move closer together there may be united in this office ministries now existing in a variety of forms and under a variety of names. Differences in ordering the diaconal ministry should not be regarded as a hindrance for the mutual recognition of the ordained ministries.[24]

It is obvious from this commentary that the BEM definition of the diaconate raises almost as many questions as it answers.

The responses to the diaconal section of BEM cover a wide

range. Some churches simply approve the definition as given.[25] Others say that this social emphasis on *diakonia* challenges their own practice and has led or will lead to further study in their communions.[26] With some this reconsideration (whether owed to BEM or apart from it) has already progressed from proposal to action. Roman Catholics point to the fact that since the Second Vatican Council (1962-65) they have instituted a new order of permanent deacons.[27] Several other Christian communions which have also traditionally had a "transitional" diaconate, that is, primarily liturgical deacons who sooner or later move on to become priests, have also begun to develop orders of "permanent" deacons. In the United States, Episcopalians and United Methodists have begun such work.[28]

Along with considerable praise for the BEM comments on ministry, some churches voice a variety of criticisms and suggestions, or questions needing clarification. Some respondents object to the idea of the diaconate as a separate order of ministry, though they have often themselves introduced special diaconal personnel (on what basis is not always stated).[29] Some of the criticisms point to a need for amplification. For example, more attention might be given to the biblical bases for the ministry. More weight should be given to the importance of the Word and preaching in inspiring *diakonia;* the diaconate pictured in BEM is rightly closely related to the Eucharist, but the connection with preaching is neglected.[30] In practical terms, the focus is only on the local congregation, but there is a need for attention to deacons whose context is regional or otherwise extends beyond the eucharistic community.[31]

The definition of the diaconate, and especially the questions noted in the accompanying commentary, point to some more serious issues of omission or unclarity. Critical among these problems is the relationship of the diaconate to the ministry of the laity. The United Methodist Church (UK) summarizes this whole problem very well.

> Thirdly, we are aware of the difficulties that all churches have encountered in their attempts to establish a satisfactory model

of the diaconate. We believe in the serving Church and we believe that the Christian Church does in fact offer service to God and to the world. We are not alone in confessing that we have not been able to create and preserve a model of a vigorous diaconate, open to both sexes and not directed to the presbyterate (although the Wesley Deaconess Order comes very close to it). On the other hand we take very seriously the concern that a separate diaconate might lead to a devaluation of the ministry of the laity, and cannot accept that a separate diaconate is necessarily appropriate in every situation in the church. However, we wish to approach this issue with sympathy and receptivity and pledge ourselves to a continual exploration of it.[32]

In various ways this concern is echoed by many other churches. The diaconate as defined by BEM is "too churchly," turned inward and insufficiently attentive to the world, the oppressed.[33] One church largely of Reformed background, the United Church of Canada, complains also that the description of the deacon in BEM does not recognize many of the commissioned diaconal activities of their communion.[34] Although none of the responses actually speaks of secular welfare agencies and questions of *diakonia* in the workplace, these are probably subsumed under concern for the ministry of the laity. However, more explicit attention to this facet of the question would be helpful.

Related to these criticisms are the frequent queries about other church workers and offices not mentioned in BEM. Why do deacons have a special status which teachers and youth workers, provincial, diocesan, and congregational secretaries, and others do not have? Why are deacons singled out? How do they differ from these other special ministries of the contemporary church?[35] In this connection it is appropriate to note that many churches in the Reformed tradition raise the question of the office of elder and its relationship to the discussion of the diaconate and its omission from consideration in BEM. Students of the Reformed tradition are left wondering if the responsibilities of the Reformed elder are subsumed under the diaconate. If so, quite a few question the appropriateness or adequacy of this solution to the problem of the orders of ministry.[36]

Obviously, a great many questions about the diaconate in the late twentieth-century ecumenical church remain to be answered. The response of the Baptist Union of Great Britain and Ireland to BEM points to the problem of theological definition in the paragraph on the diaconate.

> That the presence of a threefold *order* of ministry is really the divisive question at issue seems reinforced by the shifts of language in the report when diaconal ministry is under discussion. We begin at M20-21 with deacons as the *functionaries* assisting the bishop. At M22 we hear of "diaconal aspects and *functions*." On reaching M24 we hear of *deacons* who have lost the *function* of diaconal witness. By the time we reach M31 we are presented with a vision of deacons who on the one hand are diaconal in *function* (servants in the world) but who in the next few sentences become omnibus *functionaries* liturgically, catechetically, *et* innumerably *al.* This confusion suggests a striving to justify a threefold *order*.[37]

The Church of North India, a union church with strongly Reformed background, suggests that the Reformed tradition may have something important to contribute to as well as learn from the ecumenical discussion of the diaconate.

> *M25: The diaconate in the threefold ministry*—This section asks the churches having the threefold ministry to develop fully its potential and the churches presently without a threefold ministry to face the powerful claim of that form to be accepted. These two calls must be seen as closely interrelated. The three functions are important, but in most situations where the threefold ministry is accepted the deacon's place is ill-defined and insignificant whereas in the Congregationalist/Baptist traditions it is much clearer. The reform and acceptance of the threefold *pattern* of the ministry must go along with its effective exercise of the threefold *function*.[38]

Inspired in part by the BEM document and in part by other ecumenical contacts, the discussion on the nature of the Christian diaconate has expanded on the national level in the United States. In addition to various bilateral or interconfessional dialogues, the National Council of Churches' Faith and Order Commission has undertaken to sponsor several meetings on the diaconate. The first, in February 1987, brought together primarily theologians and church executives; the second, in December 1988, concentrated on gathering deacons in service to share with each other more practical views of varied efforts, successes, problems, and prospects.

One thing which has become clear at least to some members of the Presbyterian Church (USA) is that Reformed voices have been lacking in these contemporary American discussions of the diaconate. Recognizing that every tradition has something to learn and something to share, it is hoped that the present discussion of the Reformed diaconate might be one small contribution to the late twentieth-century ecumenical reflection on the theological bases for the church's diaconate.

Chapter Six

THE FUTURE BY WAY
OF THE PAST

Further consideration of the offices of presbyter and deacon will be helpful. For more than 450 years some of the churches have been exploring different lines of interpretation of the offices of presbyter and deacon. The office of deacon especially was transformed in Geneva in the sixteenth century, and as heirs of John Calvin, we are constrained to agree with the document that it may need redefinition again today.

Presbyterian Church (USA), "Response to BEM"[1]

THE ECUMENICAL CHURCH is our contemporary context, the whole of which the Reformed family of denominations is a part. It is the function of the parts to build up the whole, and it may well be that the Reformed tradition has important insights to offer in the wider discussion of the church's diaconate in the contemporary world. Such a contribution will be possible, however, only if we first put our own house in order.

One way of being faithful, of continually reforming ourselves *(ecclesia reformata semper reformanda)*, is by examining our historical context. Drawing on our heritage emphatically does not mean copying the past woodenly. Nor can any one individual or one denomination define how the past could or should be adapted to serve the present and build for the future. More properly, there may well be a variety of ways in which the wisdom of the past can be reconceived and transformed for the needs of a new age. The special insights of the intervening centuries must not be neglected; the seventeenth, eighteenth, nineteenth, and twentieth centuries also have contributions to make and correctives to offer. We may well imitate provident householders who draw from their treasure both old and new (Matt. 13:52). The new is the ecumenical church movement and the contemporary understanding of the needs and opportunities in our global village; the old is the theological heritage given form in the sixteenth century by John Calvin and others.

FROM THEN UNTIL NOW

If a modern teaching on the Reformed diaconate is understood as a reconceiving of classical doctrine in the light of four centuries of change, it may be useful first to summarize each of these contributing factors.

The classical Reformed diaconate was based in theory exclusively on Scripture because that was the only recognized religious authority. It was also influenced by the historical context in which it was developed, especially with regard to the canons by which Scripture was interpreted but also with regard to the contemporary social welfare practices. The classical Reformed doctrine taught that deacons exercise a biblical and necessary office in the church. Deacons are charged with the care of the sick and others suffering in the community. Although individual deacons may come and go, the office itself is permanent. While second in rank to the presbyter, a deacon is a minister of the church and not simply the deputy of the pastor. Deacons should administer the financial resources given for the poor and personally care for the needy. Men and women respectively carry out these tasks, with the women subordinate to the men. Ecclesiastical deacons may also be civil alms officers, since in a Christian society the magistracy has a certain responsibility for the well-being of the citizens. However, ecclesiastical deacons may function equally well in a legally disestablished church, since they are primarily leaders of the ecclesiastical community.

Many factors, both theological and historical, have changed the world for twentieth-century heirs of the Reformed tradition, but only a few of the most significant can be noted here. In theological terms, the most striking and crucial changes have come in the challenges to biblical authority and in the way Scripture is interpreted. The development of the historical-critical method of biblical analysis has rendered obsolete a fashion of constructing theological arguments by appeal to authority. No longer can we accept as convincing Calvin's interpretation of Romans 12:8 or, more importantly, his conviction that all of the New Testament writings must fit together in one coherent picture of church order. Thus the distinguishing of two offices within the diaconate is no longer tenable on the grounds Calvin argued, although the plurality of functions—managing finances and personally caring for individuals, and perhaps other "diaconal" activities!—can be understood as expressions of the obligatory Christian concern for the neighbor.

Although it modifies Calvin's picture of the diaconate, the new biblical criticism does not fundamentally change the essence of the teaching. The overwhelming emphasis in all of Scripture on the necessary mutuality of worship and ethics, love of God and love of the neighbor, remains clear. Modern scholars also agree that it is strongly probable that the first-century church set apart particular individuals for ministry to the needy as well as for the much better established preaching office(s). For example, reading Acts 6 as a reference to deacons in charge of relief for the poor may not be as farfetched as some contemporary biblical scholars think. The original election of the seven may indeed not have been intended to establish an order of ministers who care for the needy, but that is clearly the meaning given to the story by the writer of Acts, as Lukas Vischer explains.

[The significance of the] story of Acts . . . lies in any case less in the events to which it points than in the way in which Luke records it. For it is obvious that Luke describes the events from a point of view that is important for his time and milieu, and thus interprets them in a way which does not perhaps correspond to the historical reality, but which is important as such. He demonstrates by means of these events how the division of functions arose in the Church. Clearly it was already current practice at his time to distinguish between the tasks of preaching and oversight and welfare work as a special function, and so it would be natural to present the events of the seven, already several years before, from this point of view.[2]

Contemporary biblical scholars' insistence on the varied character of New Testament communities may complicate Calvin's picture of one clear pattern of church offices, but it can also enrich our appreciation for the many possible ways to act out faith. Awareness of the variety of New Testament ecclesiastical leaders and the historical context of the different writings can in fact help twentieth-century Christians deal with one of the critical problems of Calvin's diaconate, the role assigned to women. Modern studies of the Bible enable us to appreciate the individual roles of Phoebe and the widows as special, though probably typical, instances of early Christian diaconal activity, without insisting that this was a uniform biblical office. It is worth remembering in this connection that Calvin could recognize the historically conditioned character of Scripture in Paul's injunction to women to keep silent in church. In keeping with the idea of historical circumstances influencing church practice, we may note again that Calvin's own conditions for women's ecclesiastical leadership have been met in our day. Our rather different society, shaped by a secularized form of the priesthood of believers, professes the equal worth of all human beings and sees nothing indecorous in roles of public leadership for women.

There remains the question of the authority of Scripture: why pay special attention to the Bible, even if it can still support a teaching on the diaconate? One convincing answer, the traditional Reformed answer, is the affirmation that through the power of the Holy Spirit we, like our ancestors in the faith, continue to hear, to experience, the Word of God in these historically conditioned writings. Because of this experience, Scripture remains authoritative for our faith and practice, even if we see its complexity and ambiguities more clearly today than Calvin did in the sixteenth century.

If the challenge to the authority of Scripture is the key theological change, pluralism and church-state relationships are the most important cultural changes since the Protestant Reformation. We live in a very different world, a pluralistic world of religious societies which are voluntary in a civil sense. In fact, however, this particular aspect of modern society causes less difficulty for Calvinist Reformed church orders than for most others, especially with regard to the diaconate. The sixteenth-century Reformed tradition insisted on ecclesiastical autonomy and emphasized the common Protestant conviction that the Holy Spirit is not confined to working through the ecclesiastical; thus it provided both established and disestablished models of the diaconate. The twentieth-century context requires a somewhat broader toleration of civil authorities which make no claim to be Christian, but modern Reformed theology is in principle well prepared to function cooperatively in the context of separation of church and state. Various adjustments are also necessary because of the pluralist character of society; contemporary Reformed deacons must cooperate not only with secular and nonreligious agencies but also with many other ecclesiastical and parachurch organizations of the ecumenical age. However, their significant heritage of ecumenical concern stands the Reformed churches in good stead here.

A further point of change, of growth, is the extended understanding of the priesthood of believers, and the important perception of the increased role of laity in *diakonia*. While going beyond Calvin's practice in some ways, it is clearly consistent with the Reformer's emphasis on *diakonia* as the necessary corollary to worship in the life of every Christian. The twentieth century teaches new ways of expressing the ministry of the laity and challenges us to define the relationship of the office of deacon to the ministry of the other members of the church, but Protestant insights on the priesthood of believers and the value of temporal vocations provide a firm foundation for modern redefining of the church's diaconate and the church's *diakonia*.

So, if we share Calvin's conviction that the Holy Spirit works in the world, and draw on the new biblical studies for a greater appreciation of the variety of ways God's purposes can be fulfilled, we need not fear the cultural changes which condition our modern diaconal work. We should indeed rejoice in the larger possibilities open to us for cooperation and variety of ministries.

Thus, despite the changes in theological studies and historical circumstances, a permanent ecclesiastical office of care for the poor and the oppressed seems as clearly biblical and as practical for modern Reformed churches as for their ancestors.

CANONS OF *DIAKONIA* IN THE LATE TWENTIETH CENTURY

Besides the old, the historical, there is also the new, the contemporary treasure on which to draw in sketching a diaconate for the modern Reformed tradition. Much thought has been devoted to the ideals or necessary guidelines for *diakonia* in the late twentieth century. At almost the same time that the Faith and Order Commission produced the BEM document with its comments on the office of deacon, the World Council of Churches' Commission on Inter-Church Aid, Refugees and World Service published the findings of a consultation on *Contemporary Understandings of Diakonia*. The characteristic words which describe *diakonia* in this booklet are: "essential, local, world-wide, preventive, structural or political, humanitarian, mutual, liberating."[3]

No brief summary can do justice to this list, but a few words must be quoted from the definition given for each characteristic of twentieth-century *diakonia*. (1) "Diakonia is *essential* for the life and well-being of the Church." This point em-

106

phasizes the source of *diakonia* in Christ's ministry, the fact that service is not optional but necessary for Christian life. (2) "Diakonia takes shape in the *local* Church, for in their local context the churches have to be servants of the Lord, open to the needs of the society in which they live." (3) "Local diakonia needs to be complemented by *world-wide* diakonia." This pair of parameters describes where the church is called to serve. (4) "Diakonia should emphasize *preventive* action." Attention to symptoms is not enough; the roots of suffering and need must be addressed. (5) "Diakonia is concerned with *structural* or *political* dimensions. . . . Churches must have a concern for justice. Even when the objective of service is not political, its effect may be." This corollary to preventive action may be one of the most controversial marks of twentieth-century *diakonia*. (6) "Diakonia is *humanitarian*, which means it is not limited to churches and Christians. We must recognize that God is working in the world, not only through the churches, but also through dedicated individuals and groups who struggle outside the churches for a more just and human society. . . . Christians may discover that inter-faith or community organizations are the most effective means of service." The pluralistic world in which we live must be recognized, and secular deacons must be appreciated and supported. (7) "Diakonia should be *mutual*. Real service recognizes in other people God's image, and feelings of superiority are incompatible with this. . . . Since the Christian emphasis is on giving one's self, and not only material things, everyone can be a giver." (8) "Diakonia is *liberating*. The churches have been concerned for people's participation, but if the people are to participate, they should do so as equals." This final injunction is perhaps the most difficult, because empowering others to serve themselves requires infinite courtesy as well as courage.

These eight characteristics of *diakonia* provide a marked challenge, but they also may serve to guide the development of ecclesiastical diaconates faithful to Christ's servant call in the context of the late twentieth century.

SUGGESTIONS FOR A CONTEMPORARY REFORMED DIACONATE

The following is my personal sketch of how the principal insights of the classical Reformed teaching on the diaconate and modern ecumenical ideals of *diakonia* might be made useful for the contemporary church, offered as a suggestion for your consideration. The major foci of attention are the functions of deacons and the spheres in which they serve; the personnel and status of the diaconate are treated less extensively.

What should the specific tasks of the diaconate be? This question has, over the centuries, been answered in many different ways. Sometimes diaconal concerns have been carried out by people not named deacons, sometimes deacons have filled roles not immediately recognizable as diaconal. Listing of duties would not be feasible, but some general principles and concrete suggestions can be sketched.

Deacons should not be ignorant about pastoral needs in the congregation or community, but their fundamental task is leading the church in justice and caring ministries. (It should be said here that the diaconate must not become an omnibus category to cover everything that the pastor does not do.)[4] The function of deacons has traditionally been understood as charity, care for the sick and poor; it can and should be extended to include all the concerns of justice. *Justitia,* righteousness, justice, is Calvin's favorite alternative to *caritas* for summing up the second table of the law, the love for the neighbor.[5] Seeking the just rights of any person who is being treated unfairly is a way of honoring God, of recognizing the image of God in God's children. In the *Institutes* Calvin affirms that service to justice is service to God.

> I say that not only they who labor for the defense of the gospel but they who in any way maintain the cause of righteousness suffer persecution for righteousness. Therefore, whether in declaring God's truth against Satan's falsehoods or in taking up the protection of the good and the innocent against the wrongs of the wicked, we must undergo the offenses and hatred of the

world, which may imperil either our life, our fortunes, or our honor. Let us not grieve or be troubled in thus far devoting our efforts to God, or count ourselves miserable in those matters in which he has with his own lips declared us blessed [Matt. 5:10].[6]

Whether the task is the more traditional understanding of charity or oriented toward issues of social justice, deacons function primarily within the local church. Sick, poor, and deprived people are to be found in every congregation. Deacons should be watchful for any signs of distress in the church, to assist the congregation in caring for the needs of its own members. Deacons should also take the lead in helping congregations recognize and deal with problems such as discrimination within the church or denomination itself. Church members should be alert to aid the deacons in these tasks by bringing problems to their attention. Beyond responding to any known this-worldly needs of individual church members, the diaconate has a number of other important roles in the local congregation. Some of these may be designated as educational: teaching, de-provincializing, facilitating. Others are dynamic or relational: focusing, relating, empowering, and challenging or inspiring. The third branch is administrative.

What may be called the first cluster of diaconal functions in the local church is broadly *educational*. Deacons are the church's teachers on matters of charity and justice. They are charged with extending awareness of Christian responsibility in face of the many problems of human suffering both within the immediate congregation and especially in the larger and less well-known community. Deacons may organize church school classes on the nature of *diakonia* and each Christian's obligations to the neighbor. Knowledge of the biblical and theological bases for *caritas* is essential if Christians are to understand that their worship implies service in the world, and their daily work may be filled with meaning if it is done to honor God.

One very important way of broadening the educational aspect of *diakonia* is this emphasis on what is sometimes called "the ministry of the laity,"[7] or extending awareness of the diaconal aspects of each member's workday life. Such a plan would enable individuals as participants and teachers together to reflect on and share with each other their daily service. They would not only learn how to recognize and appreciate the many ways they and others do or can serve human need in the workday world, but they might also gain a clearer sense of what it means to link Sunday with the rest of the week.

Another significant aspect of diaconal education would be ways of learning about the ordinary facts or circumstances of twentieth-century *diakonia*. Deacons should be able to organize various kinds of educational experiences to reveal the actual needs of real people and how these can be met. Teaching a congregation about service opportunities requires considerable knowledge. Sometimes particular deacons may be in a position to do this teaching themselves, both in the church school and through field visits to projects in the community (or even on occasion overseas). Often, however, deacons may well call on others to round out the congregation's understanding of a particular problem. One way this task may be done is by facilitating the education of members by members. Deacons should know who in the congregation has particular expertise in social problems and ask these people to teach both them and the congregation about such needs.

An often neglected but very important aspect of all education for *diakonia* is training in mutuality. One of the great difficulties of much charity and even of justice efforts is that these are done from an attitude of superiority. Christians must come to appreciate how much they can receive through their giving; we must come to see service as partnership with others of God's children who may be different but are not less valuable in God's sight than we are. Deacons must know how to listen to those whom they wish to help, so that the people needing help may be enabled to understand and to decide for themselves what they want and need, and to be able to contribute to the work.[8]

The second cluster of diaconal duties within the local congregation is slightly more difficult to characterize in one word, but it can perhaps be called *dynamic* or *prophetic*. Deacons are the church's standing committee for caring and justice concerns, to initiate and coordinate the church's ministry to the unfortunate or abused. The coordinating aspects of the diaconate are transmitting or articulating and relating. Deacons serve as the church's focus or clearinghouse for helping individuals with special concerns get the attention of all of the congregation. Individual church members should understand the function of the diaconate and know how to alert the deacons and thus the whole congregation to problems within the church or community. Deacons cannot be everywhere; they need the help of the congregation to learn about special problems. Any member of the congregation with knowledge of a person in need, or with special understanding of a given social problem, should feel free to ask the deacons' aid in presenting the matter to the congregation for their prayers or active involvement.

The relating function of the diaconate is the obverse, or a different expression, of the clearinghouse function. The diaconate is theologically the central organ of all church charitable or justice projects, the way of relating them to each other and the whole body. A congregation may organize an ad hoc committee on hunger or apartheid or whatever issue is brought to its attention, but special task forces should be understood theologically as natural extensions of the diaconate, not merely optional special interest groups. Relating ad hoc task forces to the established diaconal office is clearly not primarily a matter of efficiency, and certainly not of ecclesiastical control.

A special group should theologically be recognized as diaconal for two reasons. First, a congregation needs to examine and acknowledge corporately the claims that the sufferings of God's children make on every Christian, even if no single individual can personally respond to every claim. Second, a congregation needs to rejoice in and support the work of those members who do take a lead in dealing with any problem, appreciating that this work is done also in their name and on their behalf.

The dynamic or prophetic function of the diaconate also includes empowering and challenging or inspiring individual

111

church members in their own diaconal work. Although one common reason people leave charity or justice to others is a failure to see that these things are implied in their profession of faith, another important reason is that individuals may not recognize or appreciate their own opportunities to serve as being diaconal. Deacons can enlarge people's awareness not only about their responsibilities but also about the diaconal aspects of their own lives. Recognizing and articulating for themselves and having the community appreciate what they do as *diakonia* can empower each member for better service and especially for more joyous service.

The other side of empowering is prophetic challenge. Though we are often too comfortable to remember the fact, being a Christian is a risky business, a risk-taking business. Deacons may properly encourage (or even push?) members, particularly those with special gifts or influential positions, to make fuller use of their talents. Serving the neighbor only through the church's diaconate is self-deception if it is not complemented and accompanied by the best possible use of one's home or workplace opportunities for *diakonia*. The priesthood of believers is paralleled by the servanthood of believers; both are often neglected by individual church members, but active acknowledgement of both must be re-awakened. Deacons might challenge or inspire more vigorous expression of servanthood by all members through the educational process suggested above. Church members who examine and then explain to their fellow worshipers the diaconal aspects of their own lives may be moved or challenged to further activity by that process and by others' responses. Areas of common interest or common difficulty can be identified. This interaction allows different members to help and also to challenge each other.

In addition, deacons can and should challenge church members to reach beyond what they can presently see or are doing and support them in that broadening vision. The world is much larger than we often remember. The challenges of suffering can be overwhelming, and often we do not hear the cries because of our guilt and our fear of being swallowed up. This is another good reason for approaching the challenges as a group, facing the call of *diakonia* as a people rather than only as individuals.

A third division which may be considered a part of diaconal work is *administrative*. It may be appropriate to charge deacons with the administration of the church's charitable offerings, but this function must never be allowed to overshadow or interfere with the outward-looking obligation to care for those—within or beyond the congregation—who cannot care for themselves. Perhaps the financial work should be organized as a subcommittee of the diaconate. Although the care of money must not be an end in itself, it is an important means to the end of service, and those who carry out this ministry should be appreciated. Money itself is not profane; worship of financial security is. It would be wise, however, to assign the administration of the church's general finances, building upkeep, and so forth to a group of elders or trustees. The deacon(s) handling charitable funds could be a liason between the two groups, but other deacons ought not to be regularly burdened with finances, since that task would take time from the prophetic and educational obligations which have been so much neglected.

Deacons also have a number of responsibilities beyond the bounds of the local congregation, responsibilities which are too often forgotten. Most of these functions are similar to the diaconal tasks in the local congregation. The first cluster of extra-congregational activities can perhaps be called *linking*, a combination of educational and dynamic roles. Many problems about which Christians should be concerned extend beyond their own communities. Deacons not only make church people aware of the problems but they also connect the local church with larger diaconal structures. Knowing who those other partners may be and how to work with them is part of the diaconate's role in leading the church to serve the world. The deacon's connecting function is particularly clear in the case of the diaconal agencies of the denomination, but it also applies to ties with all other forms of organized service to the suffering

113

or oppressed. Since no one person can do everything, often a congregation will wish to coordinate its efforts with those of other agencies in the community to strengthen service and avoid duplication. The diaconate is the linking organ to help the church decide when and how to do this work, and then to help effect the coordination. Thus the deacons not only represent the congregation in meeting with these various organizations but also serve as contact persons in the local church.

The second extra-congregational cluster of diaconal functions may be called *educational and prophetic*. It includes monitoring communal needs which are not being met and advocating solutions. In some cases the issue may be a lacuna in service to particular individuals or groups, a gap the church could fill perhaps better than any other institution. In other cases the problem may be much deeper, though. Many structures for serving human need, for remedying injustice, are sound in principle but twisted or biased in practice. Sometimes, however, the fundamental principles on which certain human relationships are based must be called into question. It is the role of the diaconate to lead the congregation in working to change inappropriate or unjust practices, and even to challenge the grounds on which some structures or actions are founded. This role obviously requires considerable knowledge of the rationale for and functioning of institutions in our complex society, and few congregations have all the resources. This is one reason for having larger diaconal agencies than the diaconate of the local church, and it is to these experts (parachurch and secular as well as theological) that deacons should turn for assistance in analyzing a situation and suggesting action for their own congregations.

In connection with the discussion of extra-congregational responsibilities of the diaconate, an important issue which must be considered explicitly is the relationship of ecclesiastical to civil diaconal service in our modern age of separation of church and state. Until the twentieth century, secular governments took relatively little responsibility for the unfortunate among those they ruled. Charity was done mostly by churches, individuals, and voluntary organizations. Now, however, in an increasingly secular and pluralistic society, no single religious group has the numbers or resources to be the sole support of all the needy, even if all churches were consciously dedicated to putting justice and charity among their highest priorities—which they do not appear to be. Social welfare is extensively organized in most modern Western nations, and some structures for securing justice do exist, although these always seem more rare and fragile. Most churches (especially of Reformed background) appropriately recognize these civil agencies as (usually) good in principle, if not always successful or impartial in practice. Many church people, though, do not feel any responsibility for civil welfare programs, since these are secular and can have no official ecclesiastical connection.

It seems, though, that church people should support the agencies which do diaconal work, wherever the latter are to be found. This support might include personal involvement, informed good citizenship (voting, letter-writing campaigns when financial appropriations are being made, perhaps demonstrations or even civil disobedience), or moral support to those in their congregations or neighborhoods who serve the agencies. It is quite possible that the influence and support of churches might contribute to more healing experiences for the recipients of welfare. Many social workers are incredibly generous but they cannot give unlimited time to each case. The personal attention of volunteers from churches, coordinated by deacons and the social workers in charge, might significantly strengthen the clients' sense of being individually valued as God's children. Separation of church and state need not mean competition or indifference; interaction, judicious cooperation, and intelligent and theologically informed critique on matters of common concern are all appropriate for a church in a modern state.

Who should be called to minister as deacons in a contemporary church? Traditionally in Protestantism the congregation has elected certain of their own members as deacons. These have normally been part-time, unpaid lay Christians, usually with limited training for the diaconate, often officially installed in their office by a service of ordination or setting apart. Women and men alike have been called to the diaconate in modern times, although too often the women are allotted the domestic business of feeding and childcare, while men assume the dominant roles. Reformed (or other) churches which subordinate women ministers cannot even rely on Calvin's support any longer, and much work remains to be done in educating congregations and church leaders to a more just treatment of women in roles of leadership. (In fact, this should be one concern of the diaconate!)

One regular source of a church's elected deacons might well be those in the congregation whose daily lives are spent in nonecclesiastical service programs. Some of these do work which is diaconal in a traditional sense: nurses, cooks in lunch programs, volunteers at shelters for the homeless, coordinators of food pantries, foster parents, tutors of underprivileged children. Others are involved in nontraditional diaconal activities: lawyers who defend poor clients for token fees, people who serve in nonprofit organizations which arouse the public conscience about militarism or racism or economic injustice or stewardship of the natural world. A congregation can greatly benefit from drawing on the expertise and experience of such church members for guiding its own diaconal work. These individuals will also become better equipped for their daily work when they have the opportunity and obligation of dealing with the religious meaning and wider context of their service. Drawing on a list of those whose secular work is diaconal would not be intended to exclude other members of the congregation. Indeed, making such a list would be one result of the educational process of the diaconate, the sharing of how *diakonia* is expressed in each person's life, and if done properly the list would eventually come to include every member of the church!

In the modern global village, neither the diaconal task nor its personnel can be confined to the local congregation. Whether or not there should be deacons at the regional or national level of ecclesiastical organization, it should be clearly recognized that benevolent or social agencies of the larger church are the corporate deacons of the wider body. Regular ties and communication should exist between these corporate deacons and the deacons of every local congregation. In that way the church agencies will be less likely to become isolated, forgotten, and independent, and local deacons will have richer, less parochial visions and resources for their particular congregations.

One final important aspect of a twentieth-century portrait of the diaconate is the status of deacons. This is not simply a question of personal satisfaction on the part of the deacons themselves. It is a spiritual matter, a question of the church's own vitality and its role in the world. The Reformed tradition says that structures, while not themselves salvific, are nevertheless very important. As Christians we acknowledge that it is *necessary* for each of us to be responsible for *diakonia,* but we should consider whether it is *sufficient* simply to leave it to each individual. Indifference to an organized diaconate is not necessarily a sign of lack of concern for the neighbor, but it may make that easier. "What is everyone's job may become no one's job."[9] An institutional diaconate does not solve the problem of the church's relevance in the secular world, but if it is fulfilling its calling ("doing its job"), it may be a sign, a witness, that non-churchgoers will respect when they ignore all the *words* the church can offer.

Thus, Reformed Christians should recognize clearly that deacons are spiritual leaders who help the church make God's love for the world concretely visible. Appropriate ways of expressing the high calling of the diaconal ministry must be found, if congregations are to appreciate how essential corporate *diakonia* is for the churches really to be the church. One of the church's greatest problems today, the idea that worship and faith are irrelevant in the late twentieth century, is owed precisely to the lack of a strong teaching on the diaconate and a clear manifestation of *institutional* commitment to that service.

A number of ways of expressing the great worth of the diaconate already exist. Many churches have the practice of ordaining deacons, and this practice should be continued and better explained to both deacons and congregation. Deacons also, and rightly, often have a regular part in the church's corporate worship life, usually in collecting the offering, and frequently through regular participation in the administration of the sacrament of the Lord's Supper. This liturgical connection is particularly important and should be more fully developed, since it is clear biblically and theologically that service flows out of worship. Some congregations also have a regular brief announcement about the church's mission which should be at least partly the responsibility of the diaconate and thus an expression of the relationship of *leitourgia* to *diakonia*.

Other ideas for emphasizing the importance of *diakonia* and therefore of the diaconate can be suggested, but the list is far from exhaustive. An educational program for the church as a whole is one possibility. Foci might include the biblical, theological, historical, and ethical aspects of *diakonia,* and an opportunity for different members of the congregation to share their own diaconal activities. Such a program would increase appreciation for the value of *diakonia,* as well as a sense of community with the deacons elected to represent and lead the congregation.

Another possibility for emphasizing the importance of the diaconate is special training and a paid position in the church. Much as one hates to admit that remuneration makes a difference in status or value, people often appreciate more highly that for which they have paid. Under some circumstances, especially if a deacon who does not have another job volunteers many hours every week, a congregation might be asked to pay the deacon as they would a Christian educator or other ministerial staff person.

Related to this matter is the question of education for the diaconate. Such training would be of great service to the church, especially in educating the congregation about *diakonia*. After all, the secular deacons (called social workers) study for years. In addition, special preparation might enhance a congregation's appreciation for their deacons. Some Christian traditions which have newly instituted permanent deacons have also begun to provide special courses of education. Churches and seminaries in the Reformed tradition might consider some such programs for themselves.[10]

In the late twentieth-century church the diaconate and diaconal ministries may and should differ in notable ways from the classical Reformed tradition, but the latter still serves as one useful touchstone. No changes of time or space can alter the crucial importance of having a special, permanent, ecclesiastical office charged with leading the congregation in the corporate expression of love for the neighbor, provided that church members do not assume everything can be left to the official deacons. An ecclesiastical diaconate is not the only way Christians publicly act on their conviction that the worship of God is necessarily followed by service of the neighbor. It is perhaps the key *institutional* witness to, and guide for, the commitment of the church as a body to God's suffering people, wherever and whoever they may be.

APPENDIX

A Diaconal Training Program for Reformed Churches of the Twentieth Century

This Diaconal Training Program (DTP) is particularly appropriate for people who work in church or parachurch diaconal agencies, for deacons of churches in metropolitan areas, and for pastors who will be training their own deacons in congregations which are too small to afford extensive training for all their deacons. Individual church members or other interested people in the larger community are welcome to participate in any or all of the units of the program as space allows.

The idea of the DTP is to provide a holistic pattern of training as a coherent program, with some sort of certification upon satisfactory completion of all six units. Certification does not admit the one who holds it to the office of deacon in any particular church, but it should provide academic and practical background useful to individuals already serving as deacons or preparing for such a call.

The following five key areas of academic learning and a sixth section of practical training are planned as a reasonably complete program for training deacons. At the discretion of the DTP administrators, particular units may be waived for individuals with considerable background or experience in the relevant discipline.

UNIT 1: BIBLICAL STUDIES

Following a brief critical introduction to exegesis and modern methods of interpreting the Bible, the course will focus on diaconal themes in Scripture and their relationship to the rest of the Bible. Individual assignments aim at better knowledge of Bible content and practice in exegesis, including especially the application of a particular text to the student's own community or context.

UNIT 2: HISTORICAL AND THEOLOGICAL STUDIES

The focus of this course is the various ways *diakonia* has been practiced and explained through the ages, with attention to the relationship between historical context and theological formulation. Individual assignments examine particular instances of historical *diakonia* or theological teaching on the diaconate, asking whether these can or should be adapted for today and, if so, how.

UNIT 3: ETHICS AND HUMAN SCIENCES

The purpose of this course is for the students to acquire a basic acquaintance with the various models of economic, political, and social structures in the modern world, and to learn to critique these by Christian standards. Individual assignments require each student to analyze and critique one institutional structure in her or his own immediate neighborhood.

UNIT 4: WORSHIP AND *DIAKONIA*

The introduction to this course outlines the meaning and practice of worship in different contemporary Christian groups, and includes a critique from the side of the historical tradition of Christian worship. (In cases where the denomination claims Scripture as its authority for worship, there will also be a biblical critique.) The key concern of the course is the link between worship and service, the way corporate worship inspires and directs *diakonia*. Another question to be considered, especially in view of the ecumenical movement, is how *diakonia* inspires or encourages worship. Individual assignments will be to prepare and conduct worship for the whole group so that the class may experience in community the various ways the ties between liturgy and service can be expressed.

UNIT 5: AGENCIES OF *DIAKONIA*

Part of this course is organized by denomination, with the students from each communion studying their own polity and preparing a critical report on the denomination's doctrine of and mechanisms for handling and promoting *diakonia*. The second part of the course would focus on gaining a basic knowledge of parachurch and secular agencies involved in *diakonia*. Each group of students will report critically on the theoretical rationale and the practice of a particular organization. Field trips to as many kinds of agencies as possible will be arranged.

UNIT 6: FIELD EXPERIENCE

Each student will work with the pastor and deacons of her or his own congregation (where possible) or of some other congregation of the denomination. Students in the DTP will participate actively in worship as often as the pastor and congregation allow, and observe diaconal meetings and other functions to the extent that the deacons permit.

Each student will also work in a parachurch or secular agency as a volunteer. The nature of the agency may be rather loosely defined, including regular assistance at a shelter for the homeless, work in a nonprofit organization for peace education or civil liberties, etc. The assignment should be worked out with the directors of the DTP and the agency in question.

GENERAL NOTES ON COURSES

Units 1-5 meet for two hours one evening each week for about ten or twelve weeks, usually in fall and spring. The field experience requires two years, one in the church and one in the agency. Units 1-5 may be offered two at a time, on different evenings of the week. This arrangement will allow completion of the program in three semesters. If only one course can be offered in a semester, the program will require two and one-half years. The two years of field experience can be taken concurrently or sequentially, but should probably not begin in the first semester.

If the demand should be sufficient, some of the units of the DTP might be organized as two-week courses in a summer institute. This arrangement could serve pastors as continuing education and would provide a more useful format for people who live too far from the site of the DTP to commute for weekly classes.

The DTP can best be organized ecumenically. Such ecumenical support will enrich the experience for the students and be more feasible financially and practically. In this way the DTP could be sponsored by a number of Christian communities, all of whom could benefit from its services and most of whom could contribute some leadership. If the program were held in conjunction with a seminary or consortium of seminaries, theological students might well wish to participate. Quite probably credit for the DTP could be arranged through a seminary, and perhaps some professors would even be willing to make one or another unit of the program a regular requirement for one of their own courses. Seminary degree credit would be especially appropriate if the professor in question were teaching the DTP unit. The location in conjunction with seminaries would also make possible drawing on their resources, including both people and libraries.

OTHER ELEMENTS OF THE DTP

Throughout the DTP, each student will have a counselor-friend, preferably a pastor who has completed the program itself or one who has at least had extensive diaconal experience. The student and counselor-friend will be in regular contact, meeting in general at least once a month.

Once each semester all current students in the DTP will share in a weekend retreat. Graduates of the program would also be welcome and in fact may serve as leaders of the retreat.

NOTES

Notes to Introduction

1. W. A. Whitehouse, "Christological Understanding," in *Service in Christ: Essays Presented to Karl Barth on his 80th Birthday*, ed. J. I. McCord and T. H. L. Parker (Grand Rapids: Wm. B. Eerdmans, 1966), p. 151. (Hereafter this book is cited as *Service in Christ.*) *Baptism, Eucharist and Ministry*, Faith and Order Paper 111 (Geneva: World Council of Churches, 1982), comment on M.31, p. 27. (Hereafter cited as *Baptism, Eucharist and Ministry.*)

2. See H. Richard Niebuhr, *Christ and Culture* (New York: Harper & Row, 1951), chap. 6, especially pp. 217-18.

Notes to Chapter 1

1. Charles Dickens, *A Tale of Two Cities* (New York: Dodd, Mead, 1942), p. 3.

2. An older but very readable survey of the Protestant Reformation is Roland Bainton, *The Reformation of the Sixteenth Century* (Boston: Beacon Press, 1952). (Bainton neglects the Roman Catholic reform, and his treatment of the Radicals or Anabaptists is dated, but his work is still one of the most readable brief histories.) For theology, see Bernard M. G. Reardon, *Religious Thought in the Reformation* (London: Longman, 1981). See also the general works of John T. McNeill, *The History and Character of Calvinism* (New York: Oxford University Press, 1954); John Tonkin, *The Church and the Secular Order in Reformation Thought* (New York: Columbia University Press, 1971); etc. One of the best ways into a period is through biographies of the major characters. Roland Bainton's biography of Luther is still one of the best, *Here I Stand: A Life of Martin Luther* (New

York: Abingdon Press, 1951). Though controversial, the most recent biography of Calvin is William Bouwsma, *John Calvin: A Sixteenth-Century Portrait* (Oxford: Oxford University Press, 1988). More theological is T. H. L. Parker, *John Calvin: A Biography* (Philadelphia: Westminster Press, 1975).

3. Martin Luther, "The Freedom of a Christian," in *Martin Luther: Selections from His Writings,* ed. J. Dillenberger (New York: Doubleday, 1961), pp. 53, 66-67. (Hereafter cited as *Martin Luther: Selections.*)

4. The whole tradition is often called "Calvinist," but it is better to use the term "Reformed" because the churches designated by this name form a family and include a variety of theological streams. Zwingli was a contemporary of Martin Luther, Calvin a generation younger. The Zwinglian tradition was at first fundamentally German speaking, the Calvinist French speaking, although soon Reformed churches developed in many European countries. The Zwinglian and Calvinist streams had marked differences, especially on the doctrine of the church: the sacraments, the ministry, and ecclesiastical autonomy (the relationship of ecclesiastical and civil authorities). A good general survey of the whole Reformed tradition is McNeill, *The History and Character of Calvinism.* Though old, the best one-volume treatment of Calvin's theology is still François Wendel, *Calvin: The Origins and Development of His Religious Thought* (New York: Harper & Row, 1963).

5. The term "Radical" is the choice of George H. Williams; see, for example, his introduction to an anthology of Radicals' writings he edited with A. M. Mergal, *Spiritual and Anabaptist Writers* (Philadelphia: Westminster Press, 1957). According to Williams's system, some Radicals ("Spiritualists") considered the Spirit the root, some ("Evangelical Rationalists") regarded Reason as the root, and some ("Anabaptists") held that Scripture was the root. Today there is great emphasis on the diversity of the "Radicals," and Williams's picture is considered too neat. (See James M. Stayer, "The Anabaptists," in *Reformation Europe,* ed. S. Ozment [St. Louis: Center for Reformation Research, 1982], pp. 135-59.) For the purposes of this discussion, however, a somewhat simplistic sketch of the various Radical reformers is adequate.

6. John Calvin, *The Institutes of the Christian Religion,* 2 vols., trans. F. L. Battles, ed. J. T. McNeill (Philadelphia: Westminster Press, 1960), 1:690, § 3.7.1. (The *Institutes* is cited by book, chapter, and paragraph. Hereafter references will be given as *Institutes,* with appropriate book, chapter, paragraph, and usually the page number for the McNeill-Battles edition.)

7. See, for example, Tonkin, *The Church and the Secular Order in Reformation Thought,* pp. 93-130.

8. See Lewis Spitz, *The Renaissance and Reformation Movements* (Chicago: Rand McNally, 1971), chap. 1, et passim, for a good picture of the early modern world.

9. Luther, "An Appeal to the Ruling Class of German Nationality as to the Amelioration of the State of Christendom," in *Martin Luther: Selections,* pp. 474-75. For a general discussion of the controversy over religious authority written by an ecumenical Roman Catholic, see George Tavard, *Holy Church or Holy Writ* (London: Burns & Oates, 1957).

10. The best concise discussion and the chief source of the present remarks is Paul Lehmann, "The Reformers' Use of the Bible," *Theology Today* 3

(1946-47): 328-44. Lehmann uses the terms "apperception" and "interpretation." The parallel terms "inspiration" and "revelation" come from the discussion of John Dillenberger, *Protestant Thought and Natural Science* (Nashville: Abingdon Press, 1960), especially pp. 29-39.

11. Luther, "On the Bondage of the Will," in *Martin Luther: Selections,* p. 172.

12. See Calvin, *Institutes,* 1:538, § 3.1.1, and especially 1:80, § 1.7.5: "Let this point therefore stand: that those whom the Holy Spirit has inwardly taught truly rest upon Scripture, and that Scripture indeed is self-authenticated; hence, it is not right to subject it to proof and reasoning. And the certainty it deserves with us, it attains by the testimony of the Spirit. For even if it wins reverence for itself by its own majesty, it seriously affects us only when it is sealed upon our hearts through the Spirit."

Notes to Chapter 2

1. Frederick Herzog, "Diakonia in Modern Times, Eighteenth–Twentieth Centuries," in *Service in Christ,* p. 147.

2. The development of *diakonia,* service to the neighbor, over the centuries from Old Testament times through the modern period is treated by experts in each era in the previously mentioned collection, *Service in Christ.* Another, shorter but very useful summary is *The Ministry of Deacons* (Geneva: World Council of Churches, 1965). (Hereafter cited as *Ministry of Deacons.*) Each book makes frequent reference to the relationship of worship and service. For Calvin in particular, see Elsie Anne McKee, *John Calvin on the Diaconate and Liturgical Almsgiving* (Geneva: Droz, 1984). (Hereafter cited as *John Calvin.*)

3. Augustine of Hippo, "Ten Homilies on the First Epistle of John," in *Nicene and Post-Nicene Fathers,* ed. P. Schaff (repr. Grand Rapids: Wm. B. Eerdmans, 1974), 7:504, homily 7, § 8, on 1 John 4:4-12.

4. For a discussion of the themes of *pietas* and *caritas* in Calvin's commentaries, see McKee, *John Calvin,* chap. 10. An excellent treatment of Calvin's understanding of faith and the law is Edward A. Dowey, *The Knowledge of God in Calvin's Theology* (New York: Columbia University Press, 1952).

5. Calvin's insistence on the universal reach of the category of neighbor is evident in the fact that almost every time Scripture speaks of the love owed to the saints, he comments that *caritas* extends to all humanity. See, for example, on Rom. 12:13, which he translates: "communicating to the necessities of the saints; given to hospitality." He comments: "He returns to the duties of love, and the chief of these is to do good to those from whom we expect the least recompense. . . . Now *hospitality,* i.e. the friendliness and generosity which are shown to strangers, is not the lowest sort of love, for these are the most destitute of all, since they are far away from their own kindred. For this reason, Paul expressly commands us to be hospitable. . . . He particularly commands us to assist the *saints.* Although our love ought to extend to the whole human race, it should embrace with particular affection those who are of the household of faith, for they are connected to us by a closer bond" (*The Epistles of Paul the Apostle to the Romans and to the Thessalonians,* trans. Ross Mackenzie, ed. D. W.

and T. F. Torrance [Grand Rapids: Wm. B. Eerdmans, 1960], pp. 270, 273). (Hereafter cited as *Romans*.)

6. Calvin, *The Epistles of Paul the Apostle to the Galatians, Ephesians, Philippians and Colossians,* trans. T. H. L. Parker, ed. D. W. and T. F. Torrance (Grand Rapids: Wm. B. Eerdmans, 1965), pp. 100-101 (for text and comment). (Hereafter cited as *Ephesians*).

7. Modern scholars have argued at length regarding the relationship of worship and ethics. The liturgist Richard Paquier maintains that Calvin and the Reformed tradition eliminated almsgiving from the liturgy and thus divided benevolence from worship (Richard Paquier, *Traité de liturgique* [Neuchatel: Delachaux & Niestlé, 1954], especially pp. 10, 57, et passim). This division does not seem to be accurate, but usually Calvin's teaching on worship and that on regenerate life have been treated separately and the connections between the two areas have been neglected or lost. For a full discussion of the subject, see McKee, *John Calvin,* chaps. 1-3.

8. On the kind of worship God commands, see Calvin, *Institutes,* 1:99-120, § 1.11-12, et passim, and throughout the commentaries. A recent excellent treatment of the way this idea worked out is Carlos Eire, *War against the Idols: The Reform of Worship from Erasmus to Calvin* (New York: Cambridge University Press, 1986).

9. Calvin, *The Acts of the Apostles,* 2 vols., trans. J. W. Fraser and W. J. G. McDonald, ed. D. W. and T. F. Torrance (Grand Rapids: Wm. B. Eerdmans, 1965), 1:83. (Hereafter cited as *Acts.*)

10. Calvin, *Institutes,* 2:1422, § 4.17.44. It is fascinating to note how similar Calvin's thought on worship is to that of the modern scholars and theologians who wrote the *Baptism, Eucharist and Ministry* document. See especially M.9, p. 21: "[The twelve] lead the community in prayer, teaching, the breaking of bread, proclamation and service (Acts 2:42-47, 6:2-6, etc.)."

11. Calvin, *Acts,* 1:85-86. For the kiss of peace as expression of fellowship in worship, see Calvin's comment on Rom. 16:16 in *Romans,* p. 323.

12. See the brief history of almsgiving in worship, through the sixteenth century, in McKee, *John Calvin,* chap. 2.

13. For a discussion of the exegetical history of Acts 2:42, see McKee, *John Calvin,* chap. 3.

14. See Bo Reicke, "Deacons in the New Testament and in the Early Church," in *The Ministry of Deacons,* pp. 8-13. Lukas Vischer, "The Problem of the Diaconate," in *The Ministry of Deacons,* pp. 14-29, outlines the difficulties in defining the church's first diaconate. Similar comments are found in the "Ministry" section of *Baptism, Eucharist and Ministry,* especially M.19-22, pp. 24-25. For a study of the later development of the diaconate in the Western church, see Joseph Pokusa, *A Canonical-Historical Study of the Diaconate in the Western Church* (Washington: Catholic University of America, 1979). James M. Barnett, *The Diaconate: A Full and Equal Order* (New York: Seabury Press, 1981), provides a more popular discussion of the diaconate in the early church and the renewal of the diaconate in the contemporary Episcopal church.

15. Calvin, *Institutes,* 1:724, 725, § 3.10.6. See also the comments on the whole church being "clergy," that is, the people of God, *Institutes,* 2:1076-77, § 4.4.9.

16. For a sympathetic but sometimes theologically naive monograph on Calvin's views of political organization see Harro Höpfl, *The Christian Polity of John Calvin* (Cambridge: Cambridge University Press, 1982). Cf. John Tonkin, *The Church and the Secular Order in Reformation Thought* (New York: Columbia University Press, 1971).

17. See Calvin, *Institutes*, 2:1057-58, 1060-61, 1069-70, §§ 4.3.5, 8; 4.4.2. The best general discussion of Calvin's doctrine of the ministry is still Alexandre Ganoczy, *Calvin: Théologien de l'église et du ministère* (Paris: Editions du Cerf, 1964). (Hereafter cited as *Calvin*.) More brief discussions of the ministry are found in books on the church, for example, Benjamin C. Milner, *Calvin's Doctrine of the Church* (Leiden: Brill, 1970), pp. 144ff. In another work, Ganoczy insists that Calvin, unlike Luther, does not deduce the pastoral ministry from the priesthood of believers (Alexandre Ganoczy, *Amt und Apostolizitaet* [Wiesbaden: F. Steiner, 1975], pp. 21-22.) My own studies of Calvin's use of biblical texts support Ganoczy's contention that the Genevan Reformer believed the offices of ministry were instituted by God. It is clear, though, that Calvin does not grant the ministry a special indelible character.

18. Although the chief concern of this book is the office of deacon, both the teacher's and the elder's offices could bear renewal, also! For the teacher, see Robert W. Henderson, *The Teaching Office in the Reformed Tradition* (Philadelphia: Westminster Press, 1962). See the concern of modern churches for various church workers who might fit in this Reformed office; see also the following responses to *Baptism, Eucharist and Ministry:* Baptist Union of Great Britain and Ireland, *Churches Respond to BEM*, 1, p. 73; Church of North India, *Churches Respond to BEM*, 2, p. 73. The Presbyterian Church of Korea explicitly cites Calvin and his fourfold ministry, and sees no difficulty in the BEM threefold pattern, if the bishop is understood as a minister in a local congregation, *Churches Respond to BEM*, 2, p. 163. See further chap. 5 below.

19. The office of elders is treated in many books and articles. The only extensive monograph on the subject in English is Elsie Anne McKee, *Elders and the Plural Ministry: The Role of Exegetical History in Illuminating John Calvin's Theology* (Geneva: Droz, 1988), Part I. (Hereafter cited as *Elders and the Plural Ministry*.) See especially chap. 1, pp. 25ff.

20. Calvin, *Ephesians*, p. 177.

21. Calvin, *The First Epistle of Paul the Apostle to the Corinthians*, trans. J. W. Fraser, ed. D. W. and T. F. Torrance (Grand Rapids: Wm. B. Eerdmans, 1960), p. 270. (Hereafter cited as *1 Corinthians*.)

22. Calvin, *Romans*, p. 267.

23. Calvin, *Ephesians*, p. 178.

24. Calvin saw his own age as a time requiring special or "extraordinary" ministers, and he considered Martin Luther one of these. See *Institutes*, 2:1057, § 4.3.4, especially n. 4. The difference between ages was also common in the thought of other exegetes; see comments in McKee, *Elders and the Plural Ministry*, pp. 69, 144, 185-86, et passim.

25. Calvin, *Institutes*, 2:1056, 1060-61, § 4.3.4 combined with § 4.3.8.

26. On temporary and permanent offices: cf. the objection in Ganoczy, *Calvin*, p. 264; reply in McKee, *Elders and the Plural Ministry*, especially pp. 162ff., 181ff. See also *Baptism, Eucharist and Ministry*, especially M.9-10, 32, with com-

ments, pp. 21, 22, 27-28. On the social influences on the diaconate, see Robert M. Kingdon, "The Deacons of the Reformed Church in Calvin's Geneva," in *Mélanges d'histoire du XVIᵉ siècle offerts à Henri Meylan* (Geneva: Droz, 1970), pp. 81-90; idem, "Social Welfare in Calvin's Geneva," *American Historical Review* 76 (1971): 50-69 (hereafter cited as "Social Welfare"); Robert W. Henderson, "Sixteenth Century Community Benevolence: An Attempt to Resacralize the Secular," *Church History* 38 (1969): 427. (Hereafter cited as "Sixteenth Century Community Benevolence."). On elders and politics there is an enormous mass of literature. For example, E. William Monter, *Calvin's Geneva* (New York: Wiley, 1967), chap. 5. (Hereafter cited as *Calvin's Geneva*.) See also Robert M. Kingdon, "The Control of Morals in Calvin's Geneva," in *The Social History of the Reformation*, ed. L. P. Buck and J. W. Zophy (Columbus: Ohio State University Press, 1972), pp. 3-16.

Notes to Chapter 3

1. Alan A. Brash, "The Church's Diakonia in the Modern World," *Service in Christ*, p. 199.

2. See Georges Barrois, "On Medieval Charities," in *Service in Christ*, pp. 65-79.

3. One of the more accessible summaries of the late medieval situation is found in Brian Tierney, *Medieval Poor Law: A Sketch of Canonical Theory and Its Application in England* (Berkeley and Los Angeles: University of California Press, 1959), especially chaps. 4-6.

4. A few English-language examples of reform movements related to the Reformed tradition in some way: Miriam U. Chrisman, *Strasbourg and the Reform: A Study in the Process of Change* (New Haven: Yale University Press, 1967), chap. 14; Natalie Z. Davis, "Poor Relief, Humanism, and Heresy: The Case of Lyons," in *Studies in Medieval and Renaissance History*, 5 vols., ed. W. H. Bowsky (Lincoln: University of Nebraska Press, 1968), 5:215-75; W. K. Jordan, *Philanthropy in England, 1480-1660* (London: George Allen & Unwin, 1959), especially Parts 4-6. (Hereafter cited as *Philanthropy*.)

5. For a summary of the various arguments see McKee, *John Calvin*, chap. 4.

6. Luther, "An Appeal to the Ruling Class of the German Nationality as to the Amelioration of the State of Christianity," in *Martin Luther: Selections*, p. 460.

7. See Robert M. Kingdon, "The Deacons of the Reformed Church in Calvin's Geneva," in *Mélanges d'histoire du XVIᵉ siècle offerts à Henri Meylan* (Geneva: Droz, 1970), pp. 81-90; idem, "Social Welfare in Calvin's Geneva," *American Historical Review* 76 (1971): 50-69.

8. The functioning of the chief refugee organization in Geneva is discussed in Jeannine Olson, *The Bourse Française: Deacons and Social Welfare in Calvin's Geneva* (Selinsgrove, PA: Susquehanna, 1989).

9. Examples: Kingdon, "Social Welfare," p. 61; Robert W. Henderson, "Sixteenth Century Community Benevolence: An Attempt to Resacralize the Secular," *Church History* 38 (1969): 427.

Notes to Chapter 4

1. James Atkinson, "Diakonia at the Time of the Reformation," in *Service in Christ*, p. 81; Calvin, "John Calvin to the Reader," *Institutes*, p. 4. (The two paragraphs are from 1559 and 1539 respectively.)

2. See Basil Hall, "Diakonia in the Thought of Martin Butzer," in *Service in Christ*, p. 89.

3. For German-language Protestants, see McKee, *John Calvin*, pp. 129-30, 174-75. A twofold development of ministry, deacons of the Word and deacons of material needs, was common among some Anabaptist groups; see Williams, *Spiritual and Anabaptist Writers*, p. 276n.8.

4. For a full discussion of Calvin's diaconate see McKee, *John Calvin*, chaps. 5-9, especially pp. 139, 182ff., 265ff.

5. Calvin, *Institutes of the Christian Religion . . . 1536*, trans. and annotated by F. L. Battles, revised ed. (Grand Rapids: Wm. B. Eerdmans, 1986), chap. 5, pp. 171-72, § 66. (Hereafter cited as *Institutes, 1536*.) * denotes correction: "But" replacing "By."

6. The reference is to *Institutes*, 2:1056, 1060-61, §§ 4.3.4, 4.3.8. See above, p. 44.

7. Calvin, *Institutes*, 2:1061-62, § 4.3.9.

8. Calvin, *Acts*, p. 157.

9. Calvin, *The Second Epistle of Paul the Apostle to the Corinthians and the Epistles to Timothy, Titus and Philemon*, trans. T. A. Smail, ed. D. W. and T. F. Torrance (Grand Rapids: Wm. B. Eerdmans, 1964), p. 228. (Hereafter cited as *1 Timothy*.)

10. Calvin, *Acts*, p. 163.

11. Calvin, *Institutes*, 2:1067, § 4.3.16.

12. Calvin, *1 Timothy*, pp. 229-30.

13. Calvin, *Acts*, p. 161.

14. Calvin, sermon on 1 Tim. 3, in *Calvini Opera Quae Supersunt Omnia*, 55 vols., ed. Baum, Cunitz, Reuss (Brunswick and Berlin: C.A. Schwetschke and Sons, 1863-1900), 53:292.

15. Calvin, manuscript sermon on Acts 6:1-3, f186r, found in the Bibliothèque Publique et Universitaire de Genève, Ms. fr. 26.

16. Calvin, *1 Timothy*, p. 228.

17. Calvin makes this point in his comment on Gen. 24:22, in *Commentaries on the First Book of Moses Called Genesis*, 2 vols., trans. John King (Grand Rapids: Wm. B. Eerdmans, repr. 1948), 2:21.

18. Calvin, sermon on Acts 6:1-3, f186r-v, 187r-v (see n. 15 above).

19. Calvin, *Romans*, p. 320.

20. Ibid., pp. 320-21.

21. Calvin, *1 Timothy*, pp. 250, 252, 255. In connection with Phoebe's and the widows' practice of hospitality (care for homeless travelers), see the quotation from Calvin's *Romans* cited above, chap. 2, n. 5.

22. Calvin, *Romans*, p. 321.

23. Ibid., p. 270. (This is a translation of the slightly revised edition of 1556, but the differences are only a matter of a few words altered and do not change the meaning.)

24. The debate on the exegesis of Rom. 12:8 is treated at length in Elsie Anne McKee, "Calvin's Exegesis of Romans 12:8: Social, Accidental, or Theological?" *Calvin Theological Journal* 23/1 (1988): 6-18. See also the full discussion of the exegetical history of Rom. 12:8 in McKee, *John Calvin*, chap. 8.

25. The ecumenical concern of Calvin and Calvinism has always been strong. Calvin himself was ready to make a variety of concessions on church order, liturgy, and even some points of theology, for the sake of Christian fellowship. See Calvin, *Institutes*, 2:1025-26, § 4.1.12, and historical examples in John T. McNeill and James H. Nichols, *Ecumenical Testimony* (Philadelphia: Westminster Press, 1974).

26. Jane Dempsey Douglass, *Women, Freedom, and Calvin* (Philadelphia: Westminister Press, 1985), especially chap. 3. (Hereafter cited as *Women*.)

27. Calvin, *Institutes, 1536*, chap. 6, pp. 204-5, §§ 32, 33. See also his commentary on 1 Cor. 14:34-35, which treats the restrictions on women: "But as [Paul] is discussing the external organization here, it is enough for his purpose to point out what is unseemly, so that the Corinthians might avoid it. However, the discerning reader should come to the decision, that the things which Paul is dealing with here, are indifferent, neither good nor bad; and that they are forbidden only because they work against seemliness and edification" (*1 Corinthians*, p. 307). Douglass, *Women*, p. 64, points out an implicit tension in Calvin's treatment of different parts of Scripture. She says the Reformer distinguishes the historically conditioned subordination of women in church, based on "the order of nature" and Paul's advice, from the absoluteness of Jesus' teaching. Douglass concludes: "It is very interesting that in these explicit discussions of freedom in order Calvin never claims Christ's teaching or example as justification for women's subordination in the church but deals only with Paul's advice and the order of creation."

28. For Calvin's lack of criticism of the women who preached, see Douglass, *Women*, pp. 104-5. For the fact that the hospitaller also gave the cup, see Robert H. Henderson, "Sixteenth Century Community Benevolence," p. 428.

Notes to Chapter 5

1. Frederick Herzog, "Diakonia in Modern Times, Eighteenth-Twentieth Centuries," in *Service in Christ*, p. 136.

2. In this note as in all the following notes, the references are intended as examples; they should not be seen as exhaustive in any sense. The spread of the Reformed plural ministry theory is seen in McKee, *John Calvin*, chap. 5, especially pp. 133-36. The widespread use of the scriptural texts supporting the teaching is seen in the same work, chaps. 6-9, especially pp. 169ff., 200ff., 217ff. These comments cover mostly sixteenth-century continental Reformed: French, Swiss, Dutch, German, some English, Polish, et al. Other references, primarily for sixteenth- and seventeenth-century English-language confessions, may be found in a variety of sources. See Charles A. Briggs, *American Presbyterianism: Its Origin and Early History* (New York: Charles Scribner's Sons, 1885), pp. 41, 70; Appendix, pp. iii, x; William L. Lumpkin, *Baptist Confessions of Faith* (Philadelphia: Judson Press, 1959), pp. 88, 101, 108-9, 121-22, 138, 166, 185, 209, 230-

31, 286, 319; Williston Walker, *Creeds and Platforms of Congregationalism* (New York: Charles Scribner's Sons, 1893), pp. 22, 36-38, 78-79, 90-91, 213, 404, 461; L. Ziff, ed., *John Cotton on the Churches of New England* (Cambridge: Harvard University Press, 1968), pp. 329, 343-44; Henry M. Dexter, *Congregationalism: What It Is; Whence It Is; How It Works; Why It Is Better Than Any Other Form of Church Government, and Its Consequent Demands,* 3rd ed. (Boston: Noyes, Holmes, 1971), pp. 122ff., 136. (Hereafter cited as *Congregationalism.*) For the eighteenth century, see D. Dunn, et al., *A History of the Evangelical and Reformed Church* (Philadelphia: Christian Education Press, 1961), pp. 33, 38.

3. Description from the writings of Governor Bradford, as quoted in Williston Walker, *A History of the Congregational Churches in the United States* (New York: Christian Literature, 1894), p. 230. (Hereafter cited as *Congregational Churches.*) For Dutch and German women deacons, see references to Emile Doumergue, *Jean Calvin: Les hommes et les choses de son temps,* vol. 5, cited in McKee, *John Calvin,* pp. 220-21. Widows or other references to the appropriate biblical texts are included in the church orders listed in Lumpkin, *Baptist Confessions of Faith,* pp. 88, 101, 121-22, 138, 166; and Walker, *Creeds and Platforms of Congregationalism,* pp. 22, 36-38. Dexter, *Congregationalism,* p. 69, concludes that deaconesses were meant to be an extraordinary, not a permanent, office.

Joyce Irwin has said that English Separatists copied Dutch Anabaptist ideas of a female diaconate (*Womanhood in Radical Protestantism, 1525-1675* [New York: Edwin Mellen Press, 1979], p. 160). This argument seems very improbable, given the long Reformed tradition of a double diaconate. The two traditions may have influenced each other in some ways, though. It appears that Anabaptists did not use Rom. 16:1-2 as a diaconal reference before the seventeenth century, so this idea may have been borrowed from Reformed theology. See the very important confession of 21 April 1632 (Dordrecht) in Theileman J. van Bracht, *The Bloody Theater or Martyrs Mirror,* 5th ed. (Scottdale, PA: Herald Press, 1950), p. 41.

4. Dutch Reformed influence on Dutch Lutheranism and its American descendants seems to be the reason that American Lutherans instituted deacons and elders. See E. C. Nelson, et al., eds., *The Lutherans in North America* (Philadelphia: Fortress Press, 1975), pp. 9, 12, 49, 52-54.

5. Monter, *Calvin's Geneva,* p. 58, speaks of the way Genevan government under Calvin's influence became "saturated with moral considerations," and this seems a fair assessment of much of the Calvinist tradition.

6. See Jordan, *Philanthropy,* especially pp. 147-48, 151ff. See the discussion of the Weber thesis, as conveniently summarized in Robert W. Green, ed., *Protestantism and Capitalism: The Weber Thesis and Its Critics* (Boston: D. C. Heath, 1959). A fascinating new perspective on this whole argument was brought to my attention by my colleague Max L. Stackhouse, who loaned me Colin Campbell, *The Romantic Ethic and the Spirit of Modern Consumerism* (Oxford: Basil Blackwell, 1987). For Weber, the spirit of capitalism is the rational organization of production, not any particular way of using the profits of that efficiency. In bald terms, Campbell's thesis is that the Romantic movement (not Calvinism or Protestantism) is responsible for the consumer mentality. The distinction is between the intellectual grounds for rationally organized production and the cultural orientation which determined the way the rationally earned profits were spent on human pleasure.

7. Walker, *Congregational Churches,* pp. 229-30, writes at the end of the nineteenth century: "Like the pastorate, the diaconate has survived to the present day as a characteristic of American Congregationalism. But its duties early became somewhat more restricted in practice than the 'Cambridge Platform' implies. The salaries of the ministers came speedily to be generally raised by taxation; church poor were few, especially in hard-working rural New England; and when Cotton Mather published his 'Ratio Disciplinae,' he could say that the reason why the early custom of ordination had been extensively abandoned was 'because in many of our Churches, the Deacons do little other Work, than provide the Elements for the Eucharist; and a solemn Ordination to nothing but this, appears hardly a Congruity.' The statement is still largely true, though the more democratic nature of modern Congregationalism, the development of social meetings for prayer and conference, and the disappearance of all other ministerial officers save the pastor, have given the deacons a place since Cotton Mather's time as the minister's most efficient aids in church administration, — a place not theirs in early New England."

Ernest T. Thompson, *Presbyterians in the South, Vol. 1: 1607-1861* (Richmond: John Knox Press, 1963), pp. 520-22, discusses early Presbyterian practice. (Hereafter cited as *Presbyterians: Vol. 1.*) Some churches in the eighteenth century had deacons, some did not. Leonard Trinterud, *The Forming of an American Tradition* (Philadelphia: Westminster Press, 1944), p. 299, discusses the dissatisfaction of some presbyteries with the 1786 draft of a constitution for the Presbyterian Church because it gave no explicit instructions on the election and ordination of elders and deacons. The plan of 1787 provided for election by any method the congregation chose. James B. Scouller, "A History of the United Presbyterian Church of North America," in vol. 11 of the American Society of Church History Series (New York: Charles Scribner's Sons, 1893), p. 217, points to a question presented to a synod in 1824 regarding whether a congregation was complete without deacons. The matter was indefinitely postponed, with the prevailing idea being that all lower offices are included in higher ones and deacons evolved only when that was necessary, so each congregation should be free to decide when it was necessary to evolve the diaconate out of the office of ruling elder.

8. Thompson, *Presbyterians: Vol. 1,* pp. 520-22, after indicating that not all churches had deacons, says there was considerable argument regarding the duties of deacons when they were in fact elected, since care for the poor and care for church finances were often divided. "The duties of the deacons, it is evident, were still to be determined. In the South they would finally be given responsibility for the church's temporal affairs as a whole, but their concern for the poor would remain merely nominal" (p. 522). Throughout this time, elders handled much of the work understood as diaconal. Thompson continues the story in *Presbyterians in the South, Vol. 2: 1861-1890* (Richmond: John Knox Press, 1973), pp. 415ff. The office of deacons often dropped out in Scotland, Northern Ireland, and the United States. Deacons became more common in North America in the 1840s, though many churches still had none. Although the Constitution of 1879 (Presbyterian Church in the United States) gave deacons more responsibilities, arguments about the functions of the diaconate went on. Some examples are disputes about whether deacons handled all monies or only cared

for the poor, what trustees did, etc. In fact, despite some strong suggestions that deacons be given more clear, biblical, and significant roles, most diaconal duties continued to be carried out by elders. (Thompson's third volume, *Presbyterians in the South, Vol. 3: 1890-1972* [Richmond: John Knox Press, 1973], pp. 477-79, indicates that the confusion was still present in the twentieth century, though there were greater efforts to try to clarify the role of deacons. The most significant change was the admission of women to the diaconate in 1962.)

Congregationalists rejected the Presbyterian idea of ruling elders. How this rejection affected the idea of the diaconate is not completely clear, but it appears that some presbyterial duties such as traditional elders had held were sometimes given to deacons. Other church officers, such as a clerk, a treasurer, and various committees, were elected. See Dexter, *Congregationalism*, pp. 110ff., 132ff., 136ff. See also the comment of Walker, *Congregational Churches*, quoted in n. 7 above.

Baptists also were not always clear on the precise functions of deacons. See Lumpkin, *Baptist Confessions of Faith*, pp. 365, 375, 409. In the modern Baptist tradition, as among Presbyterians and Congregationalists, those called "deacons" appear to have combined the duties of the classical elder and deacon. See K. L. Garrison, *I Am — by the Grace of God — a Deacon* (Boston: Hutcheson, 1976). See also F. A. Agar, *The Deacon at Work* (Philadelphia: Judson Press, 1923), especially pp. 39-40. It is interesting to note that Agar denies that Acts 6:1-6 refers to deacons, and says that "the seven here selected were specifically detailed to perform merely the mechanical and secondary task of distributing to the needs of the widows" (p. 9).

For the French Reformed tendency not to distinguish deacons and elders as clearly as Calvin did, see references cited in McKee, *John Calvin*, p. 134n.54.

9. The problem of the development and role of trustees is complicated. A few comments are possible. Thompson, *Presbyterians: Vol. 1*, pp. 520-21, notes that trustees, deacons, and others shared responsibility for financial matters. For example, New Side Synod of New York ruled in 1752 that congregations could have trustees or committees to care for public money if deacons were left to manage what was collected for the Lord's table and the poor. More and more church finances were carried by semi-ecclesiastical trustees in the northern Presbyterian church, while the southern church usually gave these duties to elders. Many Baptist and Congregational churches, like early Presbyterians, developed the practice of having trustees. Trustees' duties and relationships to other offices were (and still are) not uniform. In *The Deacon at Work*, pp. 29-30, F. A. Agar speaks of deacons' spiritual qualities and trustees' good business sense. Congregationalists Atkins and Fagley indicate that their present trustees have responsibilities somewhat like the traditional Reformed elders (G. G. Atkins and F. L. Fagley, *History of American Congregationalism* [Boston: Pilgrim Press, 1942], p. 297). The definition of the diaconate can only be fully worked out when the roles of the other church offices are clarified, but efforts at defining the diaconate should help in the overall process. For French Reformed, see the example in McKee, *John Calvin*, p. 98n.16.

10. The revivals of the eighteenth century are best known in North America as the First Great Awakening. The key names are Jonathan Edwards, George Whitefield, and Gilbert Tennent. The parallel English movement is associated

with the names of the Wesley brothers (founders of Methodism) and the Clapham Sect of the Church of England, one of whose members was William Wilberforce. Slightly earlier, the related awakening in Germany is often called Pietism and associated with the names of P. J. Spener and A. H. Francke, Ludwig von Zinzendorf and the Moravians. The nineteenth-century movement is called the Second Great Awakening in North America, and one of the best-known names is Charles G. Finney. For North American readers, the context and major features of these revivals can be found in the survey by Sydney Ahlstrom, *A Religious History of the American People* (New Haven: Yale University Press, 1971), especially chaps. 17, 18, 20, 26, 27.

11. Timothy L. Smith, *Revivalism and Social Reform in Mid-Nineteenth-Century America* (New York/Nashville: Abingdon Press, 1957), p. 8. See also the intriguing paradigm of the relationship of revival and reform in William G. McLoughlin, *Revivals, Awakenings, and Reform* (Chicago: University of Chicago Press, 1978).

12. See Elsie Anne McKee, "Conviction: Conquered by Truth—Alexandre Vinet on Religious Liberty and Separation of Church and State," *Journal of Church and State* 28 (Winter 1986): 95-106.

13. See the best-known example, Walter Rauschenbusch, *Christianity and the Social Crisis* (New York: Macmillan, 1907); idem, *A Theology for the Social Gospel* (New York: Macmillan, 1917). See also C. H. Hopkins, *The Rise of the Social Gospel in American Protestantism, 1865-1915* (New Haven: Yale University Press, 1940); R. C. White and C. H. Hopkins, *The Social Gospel: Religion and Reform in Changing America* (Philadelphia: Temple University Press, 1976).

14. For example, for many years missionary societies in Europe were organizations without official ecclesiastical connection, although in the United States this evangelical facet of revivalism was soon reintegrated into church structures. See J. C. Smith, "Ecumenical Diakonia," in *Service in Christ*, p. 223, who suggests that the closer connection of missionary societies with the churches in North America may have contributed to the way service and evangelism were drawn together again more quickly in these churches.

15. For a recent biographical study of Chalmers, see S. J. Brown, *Thomas Chalmers and the Godly Commonwealth in Scotland* (New York: Oxford University Press, 1982).

16. For examples, see Frederick S. Weiser, *(1884-1984) To Serve the Lord and His People: Celebrating the Heritage of a Century of Lutheran Deaconesses in America* (Gladwyne, PA: Deaconess Community of the Lutheran Church in America, 1984); Committee on Deaconess and Home Missionary Service, *Deaconesses and Home Missionaries: Celebrating God's Call* (United Methodist Church General Board of Global Ministries, 1988).

17. See Frederick Herzog, "Diakonia in Modern Times, Eighteenth–Twentieth Centuries," in *Service in Christ*, pp. 135-50; and J. L. M. Haire, "Diakonia in the Reformed Churches Today," in ibid., p. 181. See also n. 32 below.

18. The standard histories of the movement in Protestant (and Orthodox) communions are Ruth Rouse and S. C. Neill, *A History of the Ecumenical Movement, 1517-1948* (Philadelphia: Westminster Press, 1954); H. E. Fey, ed., *The Ecumenical Advance: A History of the Ecumenical Movement, Vol. 2, 1948-1968* (Philadelphia: Westminster Press, 1970); S. M. Cavert, *The American Churches in*

the Ecumenical Movement, 1900-1968 (New York: Association Press, 1968). The twentieth-century Roman Catholic participation in ecumenical dialogue and activities is particularly associated with the Second Vatican Council (1962-65), and the official documents of this council are an important source for the wider ecumenical discussion. See Walter M. Abbott, ed., *The Documents of Vatican II* (New York: America Press, 1966).

19. The metaphor of the body is traditional biblical language, as in Rom. 12:4ff.; 1 Cor. 12:12ff.; Eph. 4:4ff. Calvin uses "engrafted" into Christ, *Institutes*, 1:537, § 3.1.1 (with reference to Rom. 11:17).

20. For example, see D. M. Mackinnon, "Some Reflections on Secular Diakonia," in *Service in Christ*, pp. 190-98.

21. *Baptism, Eucharist and Ministry*, pp. 20ff.

22. Ibid., M.24, p. 25.

23. Ibid., M.31, p. 27.

24. Ibid., commentary on M.31, p. 27.

25. For example, see the Churches of Christ in Australia, *Churches Respond to BEM*, 2, p. 272; Union of Welsh Independents, *Churches Respond to BEM*, 3, p. 280.

26. See the responses of the Anglican Church of the Southern Cone, *Churches Respond to BEM*, 1, p. 60; Scottish Episcopal Church, Episcopal Church (USA), Church of the Province of New Zealand, Presbyterian Church in Canada, United Methodist Church (USA), Methodist Church (UK), Mission Covenant Church of Sweden, *Churches Respond to BEM*, 2, pp. 54, 60, 67, 156, 196, 216, 322; Orthodox Church in America, Church of England, Church in Wales, Evangelical-Lutheran Church of Finland, Lutheran Church—Missouri Synod, Evangelical Church of the Augsburg Confession of Alsace and Lorraine, *Churches Respond to BEM*, 3, pp. 23-24, 54, 93, 124, 139, 154.

27. The "permanent diaconate" in the Roman Catholic Church was reestablished in the Vatican II document *Lumen Gentium*, the Dogmatic Constitution on the Church, § 29 (*Documents of Vatican II*, pp. 55-56). For recent information on the diaconate in North America, see the Bishops' Committee on the Permanent Diaconate, National Conference of Catholic Bishops, *Permanent Deacons in the United States: Guidelines on Their Formation and Ministry*, 1984 revision (Washington: U.S. Catholic Conference, 1985). See Timothy J. Shugrue, *Service Ministry of the Deacon* (Washington: U.S. Catholic Conference, 1988).

28. For examples, see Ormonde Plater, *Deacons in the Episcopal Church* (Boston: North American Association for the Diaconate, 1988); Rosemary Skinner Keller, Gerald F. Moede, and Mary Elizabeth Moore, *Called to Serve: The United Methodist Diaconate* (Nashville: UMC General Board of Higher Education and Ministry, 1987). This last book provides a useful table of various diaconates in North American churches (pp. 52-53). This table covers Anglican/Episcopal, Baptist, Christian Church (Disciples of Christ), Lutheran, Orthodox churches, Presbyterian, Roman Catholic, United Church of Canada, United Church of Christ, and United Methodist/Methodist. For each of these it sketches in outline (1) the permanent diaconate form (if any), (2) the transitional diaconate (if any), (3) the relationship to general ministry, and (4) the primary functions.

29. For example, see the Evangelical Lutheran Church in Canada, Church of Norway, Church of Sweden, *Churches Respond to BEM*, 2, pp. 103, 119-20, 138.

30. See comments of the Reformed Church of Alsace and Lorraine, United Protestant Church of Belgium, Church of Jesus Christ in Madagascar, Presbyterian Church (USA), Lutheran Church in Hungary, *Churches Respond to BEM,* 3, pp. 166, 180, 188, 195, 130.

31. See the remark of the Presbyterian Church (USA), *Churches Respond to BEM,* 3, p. 200.

32. United Methodist Church (UK), *Churches Respond to BEM,* 2, pp. 216-17. See also United Church of Christ (USA), *Churches Respond to BEM,* 2, p. 333; Baptist Union of Scotland, *Churches Respond to BEM,* 3, p. 241.

33. For example, see the Methodist Church (UK), *Churches Respond to BEM,* 2, p. 217; United Protestant Church of Belgium, Presbyterian Church (USA), *Churches Respond to BEM,* 3, pp. 176, 181, 200.

34. United Church of Canada, *Churches Respond to BEM,* 2, p. 282.

35. For example, see the Scottish Episcopal Church, and especially the Church of Sweden, *Churches Respond to BEM,* 2, pp. 54, 138.

36. See the comments of the Church of Scotland (Reformed), United Reformed Church in the United Kingdom, *Churches Respond to BEM,* 1, pp. 96-97, 107. See also the Presbyterian Church of Wales (and possibly Lutheran Church of Australia), *Churches Respond to BEM,* 2, pp. 172, 97; Presbyterian Church in Ireland, Covenanted Baptist Churches in Wales, *Churches Respond to BEM,* 3, pp. 217, 256.

37. Baptist Union of Great Britain and Ireland, *Churches Respond to BEM,* 1, p. 73.

38. Church of North India, *Churches Respond to BEM,* 2, p. 73. See also the Presbyterian Church of Korea, which explicitly cites Calvin and his four-fold ministry and sees no difficulty in the BEM threefold pattern, if the bishop is understood as a minister in a local congregation, *Churches Respond to BEM,* 2, p. 163.

Notes to Chapter 6

1. *The Churches Respond to Baptism, Eucharist and Ministry,* vol. 3, Presbyterian Church (USA), § 31.270, p. 203.

2. Lukas Vischer, "The Problem of the Diaconate," in *The Ministry of Deacons,* p. 16.

3. *Contemporary Understandings of Diakonia: Report of a Consultation* (Geneva: World Council of Churches, 1983), p. 1. The following quotations come from pp. 1-4.

4. The responses to BEM, especially those on pp. 98 at nn. 34-36 above, point to questions about the relationship of the diaconate to other special ministries. The comments of the Baptist Union of Great Britain and Ireland (see p. 99 at n. 37 above) emphasize clearly the problem of subsuming all these varied functions under the diaconate (as the commentary on M.31 in BEM itself proposes; see above, p. 96 at n. 24). The present discussion clearly does not imply the breadth of a diaconate which can include all the varied special ministries. It makes no attempt to suggest how these others can be fitted into the BEM pattern. (It may be said, however, that the Reformed offices of teacher and elder

could provide certain possibilities. For example, church school teachers and youth workers and others might fit in the teaching office along with theologians; and pastoral counselors, church visitors, and others might fit the category of elder.) The concern here, though, is that the diaconate should *not* become an omnibus title for just any or every task the pastors do not do. That way lies diffusion and a very probable loss of focus on *diakonia*. Whatever suggestions may be made for the other special church ministries, they should not simply be lumped under the diaconate!

5. See McKee, *John Calvin*, p. 239.

6. Calvin, *Institutes*, 1:707, § 3.8.7.

7. See, for example, George Peck and John Hoffman, *The Laity in Ministry* (Valley Forge, PA: Judson Press, 1984).

8. See, for example, Letty Russell, *The Future of Partnership* (Philadelphia: Westminster Press, 1979); idem, *Growth in Partnership* (Philadelphia: Westminster Press, 1981).

9. Phrase of Dr. Frank Senn, from a panel presentation, "Service in Worship: The Diaconate," at the National Workshop on Christian Unity, Indianapolis, Indiana, 17-20 April 1989.

10. See the appendix for suggestions on what such a course of training might include.